The New Artisans

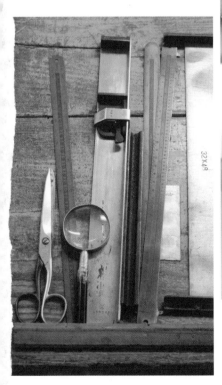

THE NEW ARTISANS

Handmade Designs for Contemporary Living

with over 850 color illustrations

Olivier Dupon

Thames & Hudson

cover 'Antlers' artwork on Belgian linen, with embroidered rosettes, by Puddin'head.

p. 1 left Traditional tools used alongside letterpress machinery by Serrote; **centre** Clay cup by Atelier Polyhedre; **right** Newly printed paper for lanterns by Jurianne Matter.

p. 2 Annealing silverware in the workshop of Anna Atterling.

p. 3 Bottle- and teardop-shaped vases by Sophie Cook.

left Suspended hellebore by String Gardens.

Copyright © 2011 Olivier Dupon
dossier37.tumblr.com

Designed by Broadbase

First published in 2011 in hardcover in the United States of America by Thames & Hudson Inc., 500 Fifth Avenue, New York, New York 10110

thamesandhudsonusa.com

Library of Congress Catalog Card Number 2011922624

ISBN 978-0-500-51585-3

Printed and bound in China by Toppan Leefung Printing Ltd

Contents

The Directory

Introduction

It is time to pull the word 'artisan' out from its dusty shelf and give it back its noble status. For some years now, a quiet but assertive movement has been breathing new life into the world of artisanship. Its leaders are not any old craftsmen; rather, they are an exciting new generation of practitioners who have come to the fore. The 'handcraft' movement they espouse has gained momentum and now, propelled by these uniquely skilled independent designers and artists, it has reached new heights. Highly talented crafters around the world have been working laboriously and passionately, experimenting with techniques and materials, to produce high-quality, modern, desirable, one-off objects of creation. These handcrafted items can be utilitarian or purely artistic, but one thing sets them apart: they all have an artistic quality – 'functional art' – and that says a lot about the combination of know-how and emotional depth with which each artisan has designed and made their collections. History, vision and feeling are incorporated into each and every piece, and that clearly distinguishes these products from mass-produced goods.

Two creative approaches are represented: objects made from scratch (the outcome of an artisan's inner psyche and compulsion) and objects recycled from previously owned or abandoned items (the result of 'upcycling', by which found objects are re-worked so that they gain an improved style and function but usually retain a memory of what they were). Both types of creativity sit at the crossroads between Art and Craft, where *la beauté du geste* is the common denominator: beautiful and sometimes rare materials; careful and high-quality production; an exacting attention to detail; and, finally, a sense of elation in the beholder when viewing the finished creation.

A growing desire from consumers backs this craft trend. Such customers wish to acquire products that have a meaning, a singularity and a 'charge of human work'. These are now the sought-after attributes for those who do not wish to live in a formatted, prescribed way. With the ever-proliferating television shows and retail concepts that promote 'interesting' interior designs, 'never before seen' brands and 'do it yourself' ideas, our homes and even our personal appearance have become targets for a 'let's try to be unique' approach.

In my own career as an international buyer and retailer, I have witnessed first-hand how strongly many people crave inspirational, quirky and affordable objects as a way of feeling different and special, and as a means of accessing a sense of a 'made to measure' quality in their everyday lives. We only need to look at the numerous blogs dedicated to anything beautiful and handmade to see their ever-growing popularity and influence. There surely must be an element of nostalgia, too – a longing for a time when everyday objects were handmade (and of a quality that only a handcrafting process could provide), when they were not so immediately disposable (indeed, they would get better with time and usage, and could even be kept for a whole lifetime), and when they were precious and prized by comparison with the current over-availability of products churned out by factories.

There was once a time when you knew who made your spoons and cups, who spent hours crafting your necklace to perfection, who poured their soul into an artwork for your wall. This book reconciles

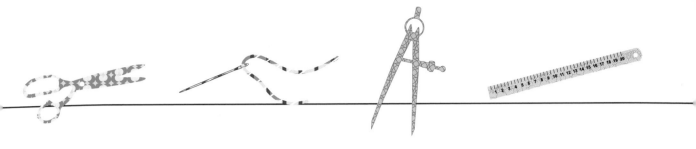

these folk memories with our modern everyday life. It is for people who worship one-of-a-kind, handmade, up-to-date wonders, and it is a celebration of a living and thriving community that glorifies its craft heritage and values its own work ethic, avant-garde sensibility and dynamic achievement.

When meaning, imagination and excellence are bound together, you know that you are standing before an artisan's work. Their objects – both familiar and surprising – beautify our homes and embellish our appearance. They represent the epitome of customization, a love declaration: an object made for you, just for you. Behind each creation, there is an artist or designer whose skills promote old techniques brought up to date for modern times, and whose technical prowess and years of experimentation have helped them master the behaviour and character of each of their materials of choice. The deceptive fragility of paper, the multifunctional capabilities of textiles, the malleability of certain precious metals, the pliability of some woods, the free spirit of ceramics and the optical virtues of glass: each of these materials has a spellbinding quality that crystallizes each artisan's devotion to their craft. Just listen to how they describe their 'job' and you will realize how profound is their conviction and dedication to their art. To them it is not a job but a lifelong passion and commitment, which keeps them challenged and creatively vitalized. No matter where they are from, the seventy-five artisans who have participated in the book all share this attitude. There is no difference between them in the care and ambition with which they approach their craft and produce unique pieces. Even if they advocate the revival of a particular local technique – Ukrainian or Swiss folk embroidery, French fan making, Danish porcelain glazing, Norwegian birchwood carving or Portuguese letterpressing, to name but a few – all our artisans have a creative force that is ingenious and knows no limits.

This book brings together for the first time a global group of international mavericks. It introduces innovative and affordable creations, which will ultimately have everyone exclaiming 'La vie est belle!' The book is comprised of two separate, yet complementary, sections. The first – 'The Artisans' – is like stepping into a multitude of extraordinary workshops, as we meet our seventy-five artisans and explore their creative worlds and uniquely brilliant visions. The second part – 'The Directory' – reminds us that most creations, even if artistic, still serve a function and are on offer to be purchased. This simplified listing groups and displays objects under common product categories, thereby making it easy for you to find what you need, as in a rare catalogue of unique pieces.

The book introduces both established and up-and-coming independent artisans to a wide audience, thereby giving the creators and their creations the prominence they deserve and also providing us with a personal glimpse of the often secret worlds of ateliers and private homes. Each designer has been selected for their meticulous designs and ability to conceptualize and produce objects of significance. The book celebrates their quality craftsmanship and their ability to set our hearts aflutter by performing the magic that accompanies the act of handcrafting. I hope that every reader will be inspired by the unrivalled style on display, and will enjoy lusting after covetable collectibles of the future.

Alexa Lixfeld
GERMANY

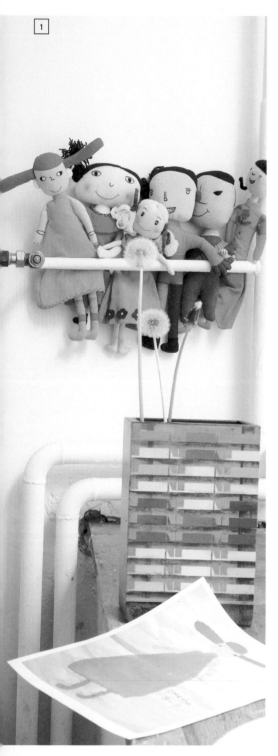

How can one achieve a satisfactory balance between design, craftsmanship, technical efficiency and fair trade requirements? Hamburg-based Alexa Lixfeld seems to have cracked it. By working across disciplines and across cultures, she challenges her own skill sets and delights in thinking outside the box. After a ten-year career as a model, she trained at the Köln International School of Design, the School of Design at Pforzheim University and the prestigious Design Academy Eindhoven in the Netherlands. She has received numerous design and innovation awards, and also exhibits and lectures internationally. Alexa is interested in exploring the convergence of traditional handcraft techniques and digital technology. She is notably keen to apply her creative processes to social projects. Expressive handwoven and eco-friendly dolls are the result of an educational programme involving Sri Lankan children. These cheerful dolls sit alongside a large collection of earthenware, which Alexa handcrafts in her studio. 'Circle' bowls are made of solid concrete and 'Cups' of solid porcelain; 'Kubus' porcelain vessels tend to bend during the production process so each piece comes out looking unique. Sizes are calculated so that the vessels comprise an architectural game, with multiple combinations available in different sizes and colours. 'Metamorphose' is possibly Alexa's most technically challenging range, showcasing the process-based development of contemporary design, the interplay of computer-aided design and the inimitable qualities of traditional craftsmanship. Of her interest in combining features of industrial manufacturing with those that can only be obtained from traditional handcrafting, Alexa says, 'I would like to further explore the work that I am doing now. This means mixing cultural, social and theoretical aspects with materials and crafts, from traditional to high-tech, and creating processes for my business as well as my educational work. In short: producing culture.' The fact that Alexa does not hesitate to experiment – creating collections with multiple layers and a conscience – is a tribute to the benefits of taking risks while making a contribution to a brighter future.

See also pp. 254, 313
www.alexalixfeld.com

1 These fair trade organic cotton dolls grew out of sketches made by young students at the Royal International School in Kurunegala, North Western Province, Sri Lanka.

2 A stylish composition of handmade solid coloured porcelain bowls from the 'Ricebowls' collection and a vessel from the 'Cups' collection, together with a silver fork from the 'Cutlery' collection.

3 Alexa Lixfeld's bright workshop with concrete bowls from the 'Circle' collection, porcelain vessels from the 'Cups' collection and silver utensils from the 'Cutlery' collection.

4 Decorative concrete bowls from the 'Circle' collection: smooth on top, matt on the sides and restful on the eye.

5 Alexa elegantly presiding over her sleek workshop and gallery, whose giant window opens onto the street.

Andrea Williamson

UK

Andrea Williamson's passion is 'colourful knitted textiles in cosy wools, drawing on elements from traditional Shetland knitting to create cheerful contemporary accessories and interior pieces'. She grew up on the Shetland island of Whalsay, a close-knit fishing community, where she now works from her garden shed-style studio space. Andrea studied at the University of Brighton, which seems a long way to travel, but 'it was a good course, so I was just excited to go somewhere new'. However, 'like the migrant birds,' she says, 'I returned home not long after graduating, and got to work.' Colour and pattern are the basis of most of her creations, and traditional Fair Isle elements are frequently incorporated. Also important is the feel of each textile, so warm wools are a favourite. 'I try to use local Shetland yarns from the unique island sheep, as we are lucky to have such a good natural resource on our doorstep.' Knitwear has been exported from Shetland for centuries, and it has in turn absorbed influences from historical trade links with mainland Europe and Scandinavia. Valuable sources of inspiration for Andrea include archive garments that have survived generations and still boast their vibrancy. Her environment also influences her, with the long dark winters driving a need for bright whimsicality. 'I am interested in things with a cheerful homely quality that can reflect a story,' she says, 'so they're entertaining as well as useful.' Her expertise is constantly challenged by the many directions in which her work can flow. Knitting can be three-dimensional, textural or simply pattern-based; it can relate to the body or it can stand alone; it can be portable, instant and done with the minimum of equipment (two needles or sticks) or it can involve sophisticated computer-aided design/manufacturing technology. 'I use an electronic domestic knitting machine to do most of the sampling,' says Andrea, 'and I make the stitch patterns using software on my laptop. As someone who appreciates the care and time that goes into handmaking, it might seem odd to be so interested in machines, but it just opens up more possibilities, especially for experimenting with the potential structure of the stitches. Machine-knitted pieces can be worked into and hand-embellished afterwards, so I enjoy the combination of high- and low-tech.' Typically, Andrea has found the best of both worlds.

See also pp. 310, 313
www.andreawilliamson.co.uk

1 Lambswool Russian doll cushions hold a 'Babushka' reunion on a mantelpiece.

2 'Two Little Birds' and 'Mr Wolf' cuckoo clocks will make sure you are always on time.

3 Andrea Williamson's garden shed-style studio opens directly onto the magnificent landscape of Whalsay, off the mainland of Shetland.

4 By combining machine-stitching and hand-knitting, Andrea extracts the best from both techniques.

5 A colourful display of Shetland knitwear swatches takes a breath of fresh air.

6 Cutting, patching and sewing together knitwear panels forms the basis of Andrea's colourful and creative experimentation.

7 Woollen cushions with a 'Clock' motif, knitted on Andrea's hand-frame machine, will perk up any sofa.

8 These 'Hang About Horse' ornaments are the friendly guardians of Andrea's wool spools and Shetland swatch inventory.

Angus & Celeste
AUSTRALIA

Leading a humble day-to-day existence on the edge of a big forest, where they go for lots of walks and come home with leaves and rocks found along the way, Keir MacDonald and Asha Cato have developed a vibrant, nature-inspired ceramics business. They named it Angus & Celeste after their middle names. The pair come from different backgrounds in terms of style and inspiration: Keir formerly made large-scale garden ceramics, while Asha worked on relatively small pieces in bone china. As the couple lived in a tiny terraced house in inner-city Melbourne, their label was initially constrained by offering only small-scale products, such as jewelry. However, they were soon inspired to include a range of homewares, which now makes up the bulk of the collection. Space became an issue as the label expanded, so the couple decided to relocate to the Dandenong Ranges, outside Melbourne, where they now live and work. 'There is a little bit of both of us in everything we do, which makes us more dynamic,' they say. 'More often than not, we each have favourite products and they are usually different. This can sometimes be challenging! However, we have learned to take each other's opinions and criticisms on board, and it usually makes for a better final product. It also means that our range appeals to a wider audience.' Angus & Celeste is true teamwork. 'We never give up and we make every spare moment count. Becoming parents, quite unexpectedly, changed our work ethic! There is no more timewasting or aimless mucking around; just pure hard work.' The couple particularly enjoy the technical challenges offered by ceramics. First, Keir hand-shapes the objects, then a mould is made. Each piece is slipcast, sponged clean, then glazed and fired. An image is created as a collage of drawings, photos and old engravings. This is made into a decal, like a screenprint but using ceramic oxides as colourants. The decal is fired onto the surface at a lower temperature than the main firing. The final object, with its elaborate colour palette and distinctive flora and fauna, transports us instantly into the Australian bush. We are treated to a stylish journey into Keir and Asha's expansive backyard.

See also pp. 261, 272, 310
www.angusandceleste.com.au

1 Imperial porcelain is poured, like an unctuous cream, into brooch moulds for slipcasting.

2 The Angus & Celeste mark is stamped on each of their creations: an artwork in itself.

3 An elegant display of glazed porcelain wall tiles in various shapes and sizes, each featuring a scene of whimsical enchantment.

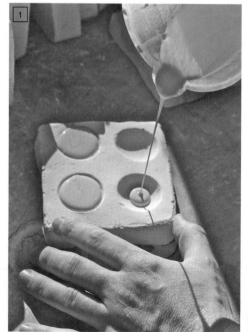

3

4 So many to choose from, so few fingers available: nature-inspired, adjustable porcelain rings to set the heart a-flutter.

5 Sweet porcelain pendants to embellish any neckline.

6 Highly collectible 'Large' and 'Bottle' glazed porcelain vases, decorated with illustrations of Australian flora and fauna.

7 Miniature 'Tea Cups' to adorn hoop earrings come out of the kiln bright and shiny after firing, together with a porcelain 'Birdie' and 'Large Round' brooches in silver and gold lustre.

8 Pretty porcelain hoop, stud and drop earrings galore.

9 Button up with these charming porcelain brooches, which come in a multitude of colours and patterns.

6

7

8

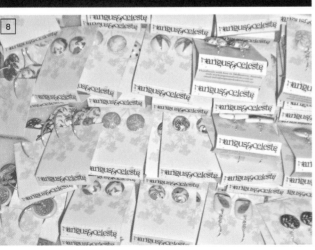

9

Ann Wood

USA

Trashed cardboard boxes become turreted castles, while ruined old petticoats become roiling seas for papier-mâché boats with cloth sails. American artist and craft wizard Ann Wood is fascinated by transformation, and that is why she likes to work with found and salvaged components. 'I enjoy using unassuming materials – cardboard, paper and other discarded things,' she says. 'The practicality appeals to me, and I love the idea of giving the humblest materials and tired, dispirited and faded things new importance and meaning.' Ann became interested in antique clothing while designing a holiday window for a shop on Orchard Street in New York City. She had recently acquired a few tattered but beautiful vintage gowns. 'I was a little obsessed with them and wanted to incorporate them into the window somehow,' she recalls. The colours and frayed feathery textures inspired birds. A large part of Ann's inspiration comes from the materials she finds, as well as the idea of smallness, intricacy or repetition. She is also attracted to the history and sense of melancholy around a perhaps once-treasured but now abandoned possession. The very challenges presented by a disintegrating garment often lead to an idea: a discoloured, tissue-thin, Edwardian lawn gown becomes downy feathers for a willet bird in winter plumage. Ann also loves the adventure of searching for materials to work with; the happenstance and the surprises – a label containing the owner's name, an unexpected lining, a piece of incongruous print perfectly preserved in the layers of a 150-year-old cuff, or an odd, wonderful bit of mending. 'Sometimes a garment will arrive and I am immediately inspired. I know exactly what I'd like to make and start working with it right away. Other times I'll live with something and think about it for weeks or months before I can begin to make something.' The latter was the case with a motheaten, frayed and faded Victorian mourning bodice. When Ann finally began to experiment with it, a diabolical owl unexpectedly emerged almost on its own. A magical occurrence, a miracle, a rebirth: Ann Wood's extraordinary gift is to awaken the beauty within decay.

See also p. 312
www.annwoodhandmade.com

1

1 An ethereal antique underskirt is a source of inspiration and a permanent feature in Ann Wood's studio.

2 Starting with soft wool legs and delicate papier-mâché feet, an owl will soon stand proud.

3 His gaze says it all: 'Melancholy Jacques', an adorable marvel handmade from vintage and antique fabrics.

4 The 'Cardboard Castle', or how to create the extraordinary out of the ordinary: Ann's magical hands transform salvaged boxes as well as textiles.

5 Inside the birthing box: a blue bird is in the process of being constructed from Japanese textile scraps.

6

7

8

6 Tweet tweet: a flock of little birds made from vintage fabrics lands on top of Ann's work-table.

7 A work in progress: the miniature papier-mâché boat, 'The Gjoa'.

8 These birds, made from vintage fabrics, have organized their own wedding party.

9 A swashbuckling mobile: 'The Weaver Girl' ship sails through the air.

9

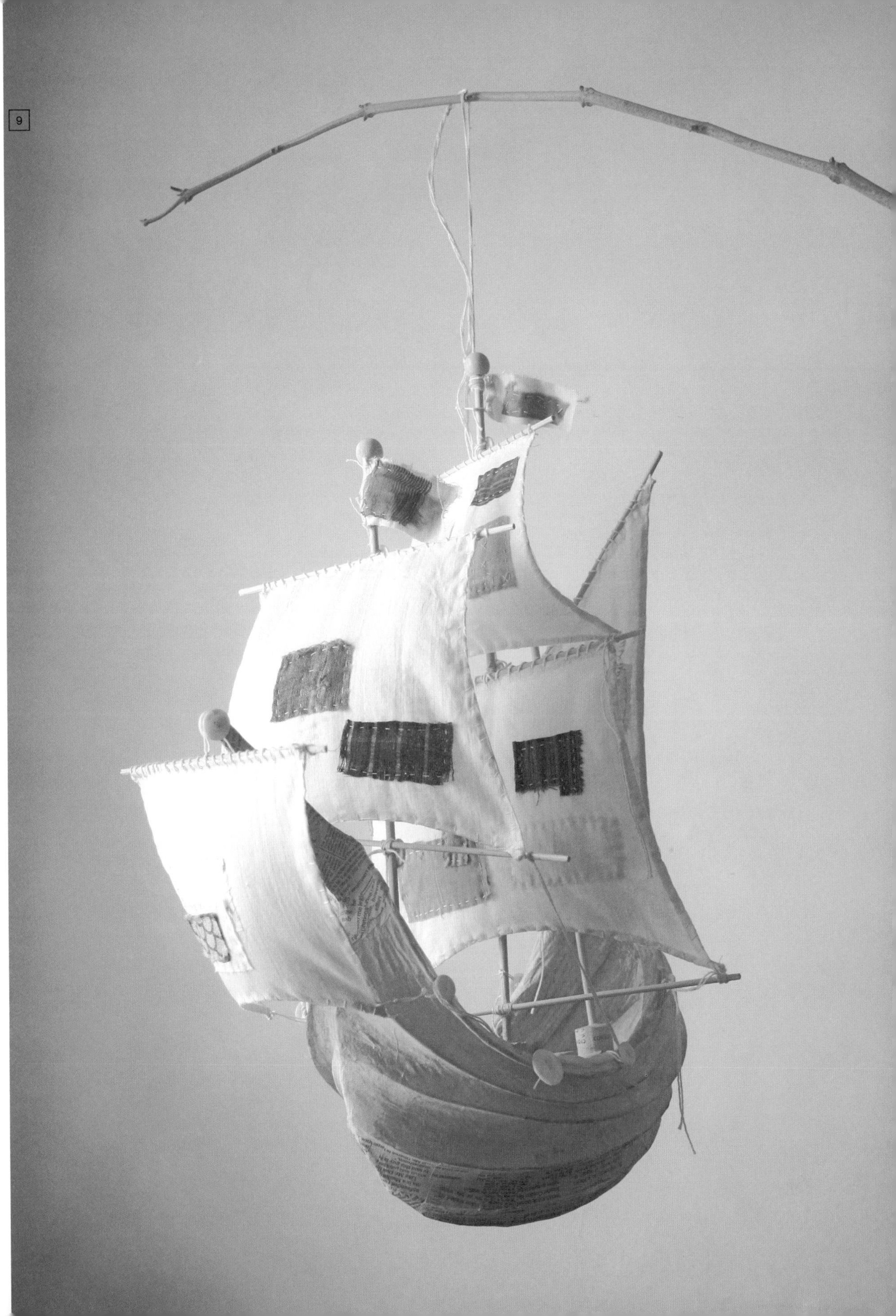

Anna Atterling

SWEDEN

Delicate rosettes, intricate circles of varying sizes, the perfect equilibrium between the sturdiness of silver and the detailed cutout work that shapes it: these are the achievements of an expert and passionate silversmith. From her studio in Stockholm, Anna Atterling designs and handmakes finely constructed pieces of jewelry and fine art in 925 sterling silver. She has always been fascinated by metal, and silver in particular. Since 2001, when she set up her own workshop, she has experimented with forms and techniques. 'Why not create objects that I find truly beautiful, without any input from others? You put yourself in a vulnerable but honest position and take a risk… That frightened me, but I felt strongly that if I wanted to develop, both as a person and as an artist, I had to take that risk.' In that pursuit, Anna developed a way of working with thin sheet metal while using the same metalworking techniques that are usually reserved for larger works. The process involves repoussé, in which a malleable metal is shaped by hammering on the reverse side, and chasing, in which the design on the front of the work is refined by sinking the metal. Anna's expertise results in incredibly intricate, dense, precise structures on a small scale. She creates ethereal jewelry that can be cherished and worn with pride, and decorative yet functional vessels that can be exhibited and valued. The 'bubbling' edges of each piece are an invitation to a tactile experience. The metalwork looks like fragile lace, but is a scalloped and etched solid surface. Delicate cups appear to sway on their thin stems, bowls seem to melt away and necklaces make us wonder how they hold themselves together. Nothing is as it seems. It is this misleading fragility, coupled with a harmonious beauty, that gives Anna's work its power. 'My inspiration is within me,' she states. 'My inner self is a place where there is an inexhaustible source of beautiful visions.' Thanks to her silver wonders, which are in the collections of Stockholm National Museum and the Röhsska Museum in Gothenburg, Anna enables us in turn to fill ourselves with beautiful thoughts.

See also pp. 2, 282, 292
www.annaatterling.se

1 Anna Atterling using a blowtorch to melt a sheet of silver into pitch.

2 Modern alchemy, or how to create a lace structure out of oxidized 925 sterling silver: 'Bowl No. 1', from the 'Corpus' collection.

3 Wear your art on your chest with 'Necklace No. 1' in oxidized 925 sterling silver.

4 A glimpse of Anna's intricate preliminary sketchwork.

Anna Atterling

5 After shaping her bowl, Anna planishes or smoothes the surface with a flat hammer.

6 A modern-day, crown-like wonder to ennoble a surface: 'Bowl No. 5' in white 925 sterling silver.

7 Anna describes her purely decorative 'Praliner' creations as 'jewelry for the soul'.

8 Frail-looking, yet benefitting from the robustness of metal, these 'Praliner' with thin stems are reminiscent of miniature Holy Grail cups.

Anna Emilia Laitinen

FINLAND

1 Nurturing nature: Anna Emilia Laitinen's watercolour painting, 'Brushes From Trees'.

2 'Allotment Garden' explores human fragility: no matter how many fences we build around ourselves, they will not withstand the force of nature.

3 An illustrator of many talents, Anna also experiments with stitching and textiles, hence the scissors and thread resting on her 'Spring Bracelet' and 'Storm' watercolours.

Open fields, deep blue lakes, pine forests and the small village of Leppävirta: Anna Emilia Laitinen was born in the midst of this idyllic scenery. She learned to knit and sew at an early age and this defined her passionate interest in anything that could be handmade. 'I remember drawing pretty postcards, each with a flower that my great-aunt had given me. I also used to listen to a lot of stories on the radio, and cassette tapes, while always being ready to do something with my hands.' Once she started studying graphic design, Anna felt even more connected to drawing and painting. She nurtured this interest with a two-year stay in Iceland, where she studied and worked. This was when she decided to paint with watercolours, inspired by the mountains, the sea and the general contentment of the local community. She also began to understand how powerful nature can be and how human beings interact with it. 'Nature can be about surviving, but at the same time it offers unexpected chances to rewrite everything and start a new story,' she says. Fascinated by its inherent contradictions – we owe our life to nature, yet we have to protect ourselves from its

4

5

elements – she notes, 'We are nourished by it, but we are only one small part of it. For me nature is filled with fascinating layers, where everything has found its specific spot to bloom and tell its story.' In her work, Anna likes to combine different types of scenery and pattern to find out how they respond to one another. In 'Forest Studio', for example, a cosy space with a delicate chair and table is exposed to a birch forest but sheltered by a delightful wallpapered wall. Anna's own daily rhythm is dictated by the weather. She is a country girl who follows the seasons, a poet who combines exquisite patterns with a naïve vision, a meditative observer who looks at the flying crows and listens to the raindrops, an illustrator and artist who draws and paints a visionary naturalistic world in which the beauty of nature abounds while always maintaining a sense of its power over us. Anna illustrates the right order of things.

See also p. 248
www.annaemilia.com

4 'Forest Studio': a watercolour room with a view, a home in which to 'paint, write, drink tea, listen to music, read and sew'.

5 Anna at work on a large-scale but exquisitely detailed mural inspired by nature.

Anne Holman
USA

Not long ago, Anne Holman inherited a beautiful wooden hope chest from her grandparents. It was filled with things they had collected on their travels all around the world. Anne now keeps many of these objects in a typesetter's drawer on her mantelpiece. Along with regular visits to flea markets, they are a constant source of inspiration for her jewelry creations. Anne lives in Columbus, Ohio, where she attended the Columbus College of Art and Design (she recently began teaching jewelry and metalsmithing part-time at her old college, while keeping her jewelry business as her full-time job). Art-making is something Anne has always done. 'In elementary school, a Chippewa woman came to our class and taught us how to make earrings from porcupine quills and glass seed beads as a Mother's Day gift. I was hooked.' Indeed, it soon became apparent to everyone in her mathematically inclined family that she approached things from a more creative angle. Her grandmother, on discovering that the young Anne was interested in crafting jewelry, started to give her old costume jewelry that she no longer wore. Anne discovered her love for antique jewelry components in taking these apart and reassembling them into fresh new pieces. 'I have always been a collector of objects and am fascinated by the histories each holds. For a while I had dreams of becoming an archaeologist and digging for artifacts.' One art installation she made some years ago featured a collection of jewelry encasing samples of soil that had been gathered by her relatives from places of significance to them. Each necklace consisted of a vial of soil, a label with the geographic coordinates of the location where the soil was collected, and a section of an antique map that was framed in a setting on a handmade sterling silver cap. Mapping and the documenting of places have become continuous inspirations in Anne's metalwork. Her map pieces feature samples from her growing collection of antique atlases. She also takes pride in reclaiming materials when possible and in sourcing the majority of her raw materials from a refiner who produces 100% recycled precious metals. As she succinctly states: 'My work combines multicultural textures with a broad timeline of aesthetics into pieces with an understated simplicity that give reverence to patterns found in nature, as interpreted through the decorative arts and cartography.'

See also p. 280
www.anneholman.com

1 This pouch holds the key to our hearts: Anne Holman inherited her grandfather's key collection, and it inspired her 'Silhouettes' series.

2 Concentration and dexterity required: Anne pierces a sheet of silver with a jeweler's saw.

3 A close-up of Anne's typesetter's tray, which she uses to display her collection of antique artifacts. The map stamp and rocks resonate with her fascination for soil and cartography.

4 More examples of the rich ephemera that broaden Anne's vision and inspire her.

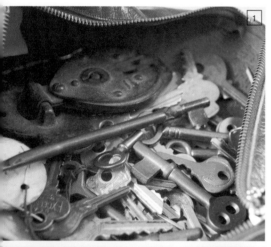

5 Stylish but meaningful
'Antique Map' bracelets,
made with sterling silver
and resin.

6 Necklace made with an
antique pressed blue glass
cabochon from 1940s
Japan, inlaid in a handmade
sterling silver setting with an
oxidized patina on the silver.

8

7 Photographs of landscapes taken from the window of an aeroplane offer Anne the kind of textures she can translate into pattern and map designs.

8 The 'Inheritance' fine art project: Anne's ongoing series of pendants made of sterling silver, glass, resin, antique maps and soil samples from various locations around the world.

Annick Krasnopolski – Les Recyclés

FRANCE

Early on, recycling became a way of life for French crafter Annick Krasnopolski. It is probably in her genes. Her maternal grandfather was a genius DIY enthusiast, who would not purchase anything that he could fabricate better himself. In his hands, bits and pieces always came together to form amazing objects, and this became the basis of Annick's philosophy of transformation. Meanwhile, from her mother she inherited the ability to appreciate beauty with all of her senses. 'I recall learning to recognize the alluring sound that crystal emanates,' she muses. All of her 'Recyclés' works are testimony to these invaluable life lessons. Originally a seamstress for the entertainment industry, Annick has retained her love of detail and finesse, and this is readily evident in her creations. Her dedication to the environment dictates her choice of natural materials – wood, mother-of-pearl, metals, leather and organic fibres. For her work, she has accumulated a vast and eclectic wealth of unwanted goods. 'Disheartened by wastage, by our over-consumption, I am now a passionate hunter and gatherer of discarded objects and materials, which I then transform and re-appropriate. Recycling becomes rebirth.' No matter what the object, this avid collector will adopt it as long as it inspires and affects her. 'I have to touch to be touched,' she says. 'It is necessary for me to have the visual and tactile stimulus from these ephemera so that I can sense their story, and only then am I able to enter the creative process.' A seasoned and passionate traveller, Annick has cultivated a taste for others and for otherworldliness. 'I like singularity, and I am particularly fond of *art brut* and *art singulier*,' she says. 'The spiritual dimension of shamanism and so-called primitive cultures is also a great source of inspiration.' This has had such an impact on Annick that she prefers to call a piece of jewelry a *parure d'esprit*, or 'spirit ornament'. Moreover, she believes that everything has a soul, and that within this lies a little seed of life and a history that contribute to the world around us. 'I am unable to wear or use my own creations simply because they are predestined for the person for whom they are created,' she says. Each of Annick's recycled marvels is like a person: it has a soul and it holds a story, which Annick will only disclose by whispering it in your ear.

See also pp. 278, 296
www.les-recycles.eu

1 The majestic 'Etnik' neckpiece is paired with a display stand, the 'Présentoir Pied', marriage of an old coat-hanger with a pair of shoe lasts.

2 Old tyres get a makeover for the better: Annick Krasnopolski applies rubber shredded to fine strips to a mirror, creating a feathery frame.

3 Annick's upcycled tribe roams free: first in line, the 'Présentoir Tampon', a display stand made of an old coat-hanger and a wooden stamp.

4 Mirror, mirror on the wall: the 'Miroir Pneu', made of shredded tyre rubber.

Antonia Rossi
ITALY

Antonia Rossi does not have a tangible workshop; she creates one wherever she is. Her itinerant atelier consists of a bag of humble treasures, which she always carries around with her. The bag contains worn-out books, remnants of fabrics full of darning and embroidery, colourful spools of thread, antique lace, needles, scissors and old scraps of paper. This quixotic collection of ragged pieces inspires the symbolic and emotive objects that Antonia makes. Her mobile poems are an imaginary correspondence made of words stitched onto layers of paper and cloth. The stitching brings all the pages, faded ribbons and tatters of fabrics together. Antonia also handmakes crochet necklaces that evoke rosaries, but with the traditional religious imagery replaced by little pieces of fabric on which she has placed words. She crafts chains out of old Soie d'Alger thread and adorns these with pendants that are patterns found in fabrics or embroideries. She re-interprets Brevi bags, the cotton bags traditionally offered for childbirth in southern Italy, in which people place prayers, or *breve*, to protect the newborn against evil. Antonia's pouches are tiny but they hold little notes to be unfolded, read and folded again. She herself was born in the Abruzzo region of Italy, her works being deeply embedded in its culture (though she says her creative drive was really born in Paris). Stylish shops, including Facteur Céleste and Miller et Bertaux, have solicited her unique talent, but she says that when she creates a piece she doesn't even feel as if she's working. She rarely plans for the end result and sometimes she simply can't stop. She says she feels 'feverish', as if she can't control her hands. 'There's a sense of urgency to assemble the various materials together; to compile the words,' she states. 'There's a necessity to dig into my secret garden of memories and give them a voice.' Antonia is a solitary and free artist, creating wherever she feels like it, in the middle of a crowd, in front of a window or simply at home in Bologna. Surprisingly she doesn't enjoy reading, and that is why, she says, 'I cut books and dismember their pages to later rewrite their story through stitching'.

See also pp. 277, 310
antomoon@inwind.it

1 Antonia Rossi's delicate rosary necklace, made of fine cotton thread, is a testimony to her nimble fingerwork.

2 'Cœurs en Fête': fabric swatches full of darns make adorable heart-shaped ornaments.

3 Antonia in a creative moment, with time as if suspended.

4 The seamstress Antonia
using little scissors to help
her finish a tiny 'Brevi'
pouch.

5 The hand-crocheted 'Brevi'
bag is the perfect place to
keep a secret note.

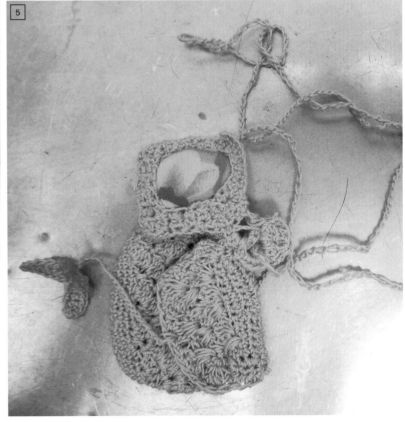

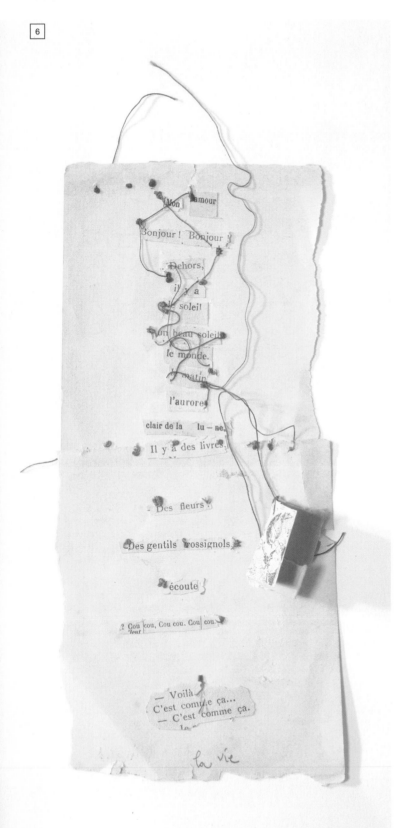

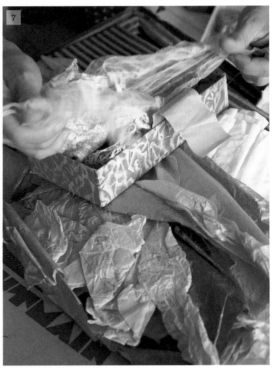

6 One of Antonia's mobile poems: an ode to a loved one, a declaration to hold and behold.

7 Antonia's treasure trove: boxes full of antique fabric remnants, embroideries and keepsakes.

8 A fine assemblage of paper scraps and fabric stitched together with book cuttings to create a touching mobile poem: 'My love, I have picked a flower for you'.

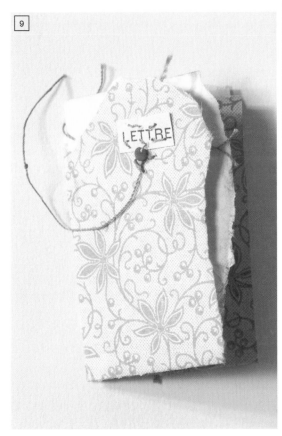

9 Pages torn from various old books are stitched together to compose a stunning new work of art.

10 Bundles of cloth, skeins of silky thread and old leather suitcases comprise Antonia's itinerant workshop.

11 Old books await deconstruction before their rebirth as poetic artworks.

Atelier Polyhedre

FRANCE

'Knowledgeable' and 'playful' are the two words that best describe Atelier Polyhedre's approach. Combining tradition and innovation, this Nantes-based studio has developed a unique way of working with ceramics, conceiving odd and unusual objects. The workshop was founded in 2004 by Baptiste Ymonet, and he was joined three years later by Vincent Jousseaume. Sources of inspiration for the two troublemaking ceramicists include anatomy, medical science and everyday objects. The pair are also inspired by pure chance. 'We get ideas while talking. One thing leads to another; we figure out a shape. It feels as if we use vocabulary more than drawings for our creative process. Words enable us to sketch an idea and to interpret the idea directly onto the material.' All of their collections – from the prototypes, made from plaster or dirt, to the finished objects – are designed and made in the workshop. Moulds are created once the object is finished, and copies are then produced by stamping and by use of barbotine (slip or liquid clay). Each individual piece, however, is unique, and production is limited to a small run. All of the atelier's extraordinary products are the result of technical challenges that require the bending of rules (the duo use kitchen utensils to obtain certain shapes) and a fair bit of experimentation (they often combine minimalist rigour with baroque quirkiness, or the geometric with the organic). 'Some of our creations are more technical, almost mathematical, such as the "Hermano" plate, for which we plan ahead. Others are more free, no technical discussion before, as with the "Chantilly" series: we just dream an object and try to produce it.' The pair twist aesthetic codes, walk on the wild side of style, and project humour onto their objects. However, they always maintain a solid quality and exquisite craftsmanship. Their 'Bombes' collection is a perfect representation of why Atelier Polyhedre is so sought after. Based on seventeenth- and eighteenth-century etchings depicting 'utopian bombs', the atelier's 'Bombes' retain an ominous look while being plainly decorative. The sphere recalls a cannonball, but the ornamentation is the twist: an organic representation of a virus, a pimple or a striking detail. In Atelier Polyhedre's world, ceramics are explosive, whipped, twisted, victims of subsidence or simply original. The duo's irreverence is reinventing the art of earthenware.

See also pp. 1, 256, 264
www.polyhedre.com

1 Laboratory technicians or mad professors? The Atelier Polyhedre duo infuse humour into all aspects of their ceramic endeavours.

2 An army of plaster models and shapes that are used to create moulds.

3 Surprise! A vase about to be removed from the plaster mould in which it was formed by pouring in liquid clay.

7

8

4 Ornamental details previously applied onto a lid are now deburred with a scalpel.

5 It's getting hot in here: the flamboyant 'Assiette Burning Buffet' in faience with a white glaze.

6 The shelves in the 'research centre' hold study artifacts, trials and inspirational items.

7 'La Baronne Bombe' undressed: facets of its production include liquid clay spilling out of moulds, a plain round lid waiting to be embellished with details, and the two half-moulds of the Bombe's spikes.

8 Truly bombastic: piercings, spikes, nipples and pimples adorn these subversive 'Pustula Bombes' in faience with a white glaze.

Atelier R. Bernier

FRANCE

The evocative names of this contemporary line of homewares and accessories – 'Zig, Boom!', 'Fleurs pompon d'Islande' and 'Trophée de Chasse', to name but a few – channel perfectly the idea of vibrant colour, stylish design and subtle quirkiness: a very French proposition. Graphic designer Romain Bernier founded his eponymous atelier in 2004 as a way of applying his graphic design skills to interior decor. He started with a line of lighting, whose screenprinted shades displayed an elegant array of treetops, complete with flying birds. The 'Oiseaux des Villes' collection was an immediate success and could be found in many trendsetting shops. This promising start enabled Romain to launch a larger-scale line: a wooden coffee table that could be pyro-engraved, a punched-metal dining table that could be embroidered, more shades and pendant lights in various shapes and patterns, colourful plush cushions, wall stickers, unisex bags and little accessories. Today the collection revolves largely around the elaboration of unique textile prints. Romain has developed a preference for fabrics, as 'they give more room for the use of colours and patterns. Textile is a rich material, and I have found that no other can help me get the results I want.' The atelier's exclusive patterns and cotton prints are so inventive that they give the brand a unique visual identity. Inspired by the three spheres of the organic, the mineral and the animal, the style of each print is defined by the choice of colours, which – strong or soft, depending on the seasons – are always harmonious when blended in sophisticated patterns. The prints are utilized for decorative homeware items and fashion accessories, and are also sold by the metre: a good way to enjoy the patterns both in the home and on the body. Atelier R. Bernier is a true contemporary lifestyle brand. All of its products are made in France – a guarantee of quality and a boost for the local economy. It is one of the new breed of names that offers luxury attributes – handcraft, uniqueness and attention to detail – at affordable prices, while still looking ahead to the future. When the pressure of the major retail chains is everywhere, one can find solace and pleasure in investing in an Atelier R. Bernier piece; an unmissable opportunity to be distinctive.

See also pp. 266, 285, 308, 311
www.atelier-rbernier.fr

1 Romain Bernier references the colours for his 'Solstice d'hiver' print.

2 Mineral colourways with a contemporary floral pattern and a zest of vibrant yellow: the ravishing 'Solstice d'hiver' fabric, which can be purchased by the metre.

3 The office/showroom/shop is a stunning blank canvas for Atelier R. Bernier's collections. Here, the lamps, cushions and bags are all from the 'Fleurs pompon d'Islande' and 'Vegetic' fabric collections.

Atelier R. Bernier

4 Instant embellishment of any chair, sofa or bed guaranteed with a 'Fleurs pompon rós' cushion.

5 Show your true colours with a cool 'Taska' bag from the 'Zig, Boom!' fabric collection.

6 Each 'Zig, Boom!' table lamp is unique, as the wide repeat of the fabric allows for a multitude of print placements.

7 The office space, with shelves piled with reference material and sources of inspiration.

8 The lord of the manor: the stylish and original 'Trophée de Chasse' collection.

8

Atsuko Ishii
FRANCE

A thoughtful young man, dressed in an elegant outfit mismatched to perfection, has just stopped his Vespa to stare in our direction. His Kermit the Frog companion perches close to him, as a flying super-hero baby tries to land on a placid donkey, a volcano erupts and a fencer attacks. Unanswered questions and statements float in the background. 'It's just me!' the young man seems to cry. Is he so shy that he needs to apologize for his entrance? Or is he simply anticipating our bewilderment and anxiety? Atsuko Ishii's characters project aspects of her personality and subtly reflect her experiences. Born in Osaka to a traditional middle-class family, Atsuko always knew that she wanted a different life. The Honshu earthquake of 1995 became her catalyst, as she was spared from the destruction surrounding her. 'It was my time to free myself and embark on a new journey,' she says. She ended up moving to Paris, where she mastered the art of etching. By using the copper-plate technique, which enables the production of fine lines, she is able to depict her characteristic intricate detail. Her creative process lets her imagination take a major role. First, she looks at the black-coated copper plate, an idea pops into her head and is immediately engraved. Next follows a first print in black and white, then in colour. Each step is decisive, and fascinating, as more details appear each time she applies successive processes until a balanced version of her original vision is produced. Various technical steps then follow – acid-bath dipping, intaglio inking, cutting of stencils for inked rollers to pass over in primary colours, cutting of pasted boards for embossing – in order for the finished etching to emerge. This is often a subtle fusion of Japanese and Parisian traits: a combination of wit and timidity, a dose of playfulness and secrecy, a dash of elegance and surprise. Each etching makes us question the characters' motives, investigate the reasoning behind some odd associations, decipher the intriguing written quotes, and most of all unleash our own unbridled imagination. Atsuko's vision is therapeutic. It keeps our minds racing, while itself providing a serene and soothing framework.

See also p. 248
www.atsuko-ishii.com

1 Who is it? 'It's Just Me', a large etching that portrays to perfection Atsuko Ishii's playfulness, elegance of interpretation and existential questioning.

2 A self-portrait that says
it all: like her sweet
screenprinted girl, Atsuko
is witty, secretive and full
of surprises.

3 A box of treasures: all the
individual copper plates with
the designs and patterns
Atsuko has created so far.

4 A new snowflake-engraved
copper plate is damped with
inks of various colours.

5 A traditional letterpress
machine stands, like the
queen bee, in the middle
of Atsuko's main workshop
room.

8 Nothing is unused: Atsuko keeps all her leftover etching scraps neatly in a box.

9 This space fighter is no match for the bold trumpeting girl in a tutu: 'Rock 'n' Roll' etching, numbered and signed.

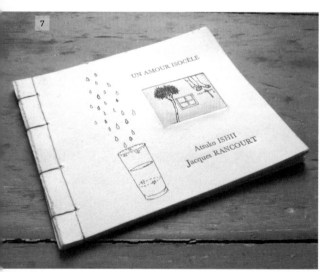

6 The 'Hirondelle No. 5', one of Atsuko's many 'artist books', made to be endlessly folded and unfolded.

7 Among Atsuko's numerous collaborations are these etchings made to illustrate *Un Amour Isocèle*, a book by Jacques Rancourt.

10 Cover of the 'Hirondelle No. 5' artist folding book: the blue swallow flying past the little window offers an irresistible invitation to look inside.

11 This modern-day, tattooed Cinderella is more interested in flirting than in finding her missing shoe: 'Come Out and Play' etching, numbered and signed.

Aurélie William Levaux

BELGIUM

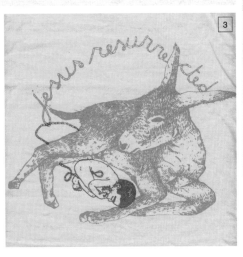

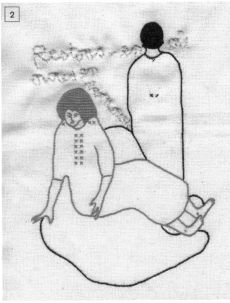

1 The female condition –
being a provider and carer
– is depicted in 'Lavoir'
(Wash house), a pen and
embroidery artwork on
cotton, taken from Aurélie
William Levaux's book, *Les
Yeux du Seigneur*.

2 'Là où nous en sommes',
cross-stitch on cotton, the
fine curved lines delivering
a gentleness that softens the
story being told (are the two
characters splitting up?).

3 'Jesus resurrected', silkscreen
print on cotton: a strong
image showing a baby
Jesus newly delivered by a
nurturing donkey.

4 Anytime, anywhere:
inspiration cannot wait.

5 Cherry blossom, tenderness
and childhood nostalgia in
'Mon mouton' (My sheep),
acrylic on paper.

Is drawing a way to escape one's circumstances? 'Possibly.' A way to emancipate oneself quickly? 'Certainly.' A way to overhaul one's life? 'Absolutely.' These are the responses of Aurélie William Levaux. Growing up in Belgium, the oldest child of a large and devout Catholic family, Aurélie has, as far back as she can remember, always had a pencil in her hand. Instead of playing with dolls, she would compulsively draw women, archetypes that she would later 'become and embody'. This ongoing personal reflective approach evolved as she grew up, though always with the same core obsession. 'I want to leave a trace and a meaning. It's a mystical journey for me,' she says. The only drive she recalls is the desire to tell her own inner story on paper. She ended up joining several independent cartoonist action groups, where a 'no rule, free expression' motto prevailed, and she published several comics and books, including *Abandon*, *Sehnsucht*, *Menses Ante Rosam* and *Les Yeux du Seigneur*. Drawing became more than obsessive: it permeated her whole environment, as she began to unleash her illustrative force on furniture, the walls, her own skin, and, last but not least, textiles. 'It started with a stain on a dress. I would draw directly around it to capture it, the ink would run and I would end up with material sticking to my skin. I adopted textiles as my base of choice from then on,' she confides. Embroidering followed naturally while Aurélie was pregnant – a way of renewing a female family tradition. 'My creative process is impulsive. My emotions guide my gestures and handwork. My hands speak so much that they end up sewing a storyline of my life one day, then unravelling it the next.' The addition of embroidery to her drawings brings texture, an additional evocative dimension. At first glance, one can admire the delicate, couture-like, embroidered contours of colourful vegetal forms, then suddenly the eye fixates on a placenta, or a depiction of a broken hymen, or the tender image of a child breastfeeding while its mother directs suggestive ruby lips towards the onlooker. The violent contrasts in Aurélie's work expose the eternal dilemma of the female condition: to be a mother or a desirable sexual partner? Aurélie lures us into her complex and troubled psyche, with her portrayals of a fragile, dreamlike yet fertile sexuality.

See also p. 251
aureliewilliam@yahoo.fr

Bailey Doesn't Bark

USA

1 The irresistible 'Ants On My Coffee Set' consists of a handmade porcelain plate, cup and spoon.

2 The hand-folded cards and brown envelopes of the 'Ants On My Card Set' are made with 100% recycled paper and soy-based ink.

3 Inside Bailey Doesn't Bark's bright studio is the stylish kiln and the organized shelving, storing tableware made to a specially formulated porcelain recipe.

4 Cups are hand-decorated with screenprinted decals before being fired in the kiln for the third and final time.

We may never know why 'Bailey Doesn't Bark', but we may be tempted to bark ourselves – from excitement, that is. The company, founded by designer Re Jin Lee, offers a simple yet deliciously whimsical and environmentally conscious homewares line: a beautiful collection of handmade tableware, locally produced paper goods, stylish home accessories and hand-assembled jewelry. Re Jin, born and raised in São Paulo, Brazil, loved drawing from a very early age, and, after finishing a BA in Fashion Design in her native city, started out as a fashion designer and stylist. Though she enjoyed working in the fashion industry, she eventually longed to return to her artistic roots. Inspired by memories, dreams and nature, she wanted to create simple but uniquely witty designs, working with functional products in an eco-conscious way. In the summer of 2008 she started Bailey Doesn't Bark – her contemporary home and life accessories™ company. She is committed to making thoughtful environmental decisions, from design to production. All of her products are made in the United States, either in her studio or by one of her independent and/or eco-focused partners. To keep an eye on quality and costs, the products are packaged in-house with 100% recycled, reusable and/or biodegradable packaging elements. The Bailey Doesn't Bark studio is based in New York City, where Re Jin lives. She strives to create designs that can be enjoyed in everyday life. 'Not only do I want to creatively inspire with my designs,' she says, 'I also hope to inspire with the principles infused in the production.' In this she is abundantly successful, and the more people who follow her lead, a better and nicer place this world will be.

See also pp. 256, 298, 302, 306
www.baileydoesntbark.com

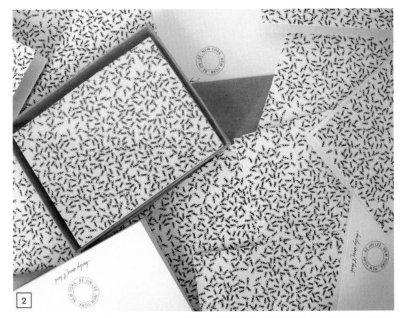

5 The practical shelving holds both finished products and items awaiting food-safe glazing and screenprinting.

6 The dot design of the 'Dotted Cushion' (back view shown) is hand-printed on the pre-washed linen cover.

7 Each handmade plate in 'The Four Season Plate Set' shows a different design of a tree transformed by the seasons.

8 The beautifully designed Bailey Doesn't Bark packaging for 'Postcup' is made with 100% recycled paper.

9 The 'Postcup' comes with a black Pebeo porcelain pen so that a personalized message can be written on the clever postcard design.

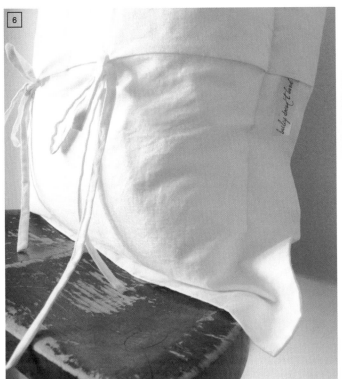

Blanka Šperková

CZECH REPUBLIC

Take a look at Blanka Šperková's finely made wire constructions and guess what tools were used to fashion them. Highly sophisticated, precise needle machinery? Think again. Blanka, who studied at the Prague Academy of Applied Arts, began to work with wire in the 1970s, originally inspired by Slovakian tinkers, who are credited as the 'fathers' of wire sculpting and who turned the trade of making and mending household items into an art form. However, Blanka did not take up traditional tinkers' techniques; instead, she simply used her hands, and no tools at all. While experimenting, she discovered that she could create endless combinations of shapes and forms by looping lengths of wire. 'It really looks like knitting,' she says, 'so I called my technique "finger knitting", as I only use my fingers.' By working with a particular repetition of basic loops, Blanka creates graceful sculptures and pieces of jewelry. Early on, she also experimented with figurative forms, inspired by the human body and animal motifs, but these gradually evolved into more abstract forms, though always conveying some distinct meaning. 'I like to manipulate the airy quality of knitted wire to create shapes that display an expressive interplay between light and shadow, which is a very important element for my installations,' she states. She has also applied her unique skill and craftsmanship to other artistic fields, including animated films, jewelry, painting, drawing, theatre and illustrations, and has won several international awards. In Slovakia, where the tinker's tradition is still very much alive, Blanka was regularly invited to run workshops at the Tinker's Museum in Budatín; she now lectures around the world, teaching her finger-knitting technique, mostly to textile artists. Her work is displayed in Czech Republic state galleries and in private collections at home and abroad. Her extraordinary achievement – in fooling us by morphing metal wire into objects that look like knitted cotton – is to have succeeded in capturing movement and life, as if she could freeze forms in a permanent state of grace. That is artisanship at its most awe-inspiring.

See also pp. 276, 290
http://amanita-design.net/blankasperkova

1 Fine wire in multiple colourways, a small pair of scissors, magnifying glasses: everything is in place for Blanka Šperková to perform her knitting exploits.

2 A dove of peace, whose body and wings are patterned with a blue sky and clouds, via the knitting of lacquered wire, is an enchanting homage, as its name says, 'To Magritte'.

3 'To Picasso', another vibrant homage to a twentieth-century master.

4 'Corals' necklace made with lacquered wire: a finely executed neckpiece, whose deep colouring adds flamboyance to the nature-inspired shape.

5 'Fractal' mobile made with stainless-steel wire: the otherworldly presence of this light, floating sculpture is deceptively large due to the projected shadows.

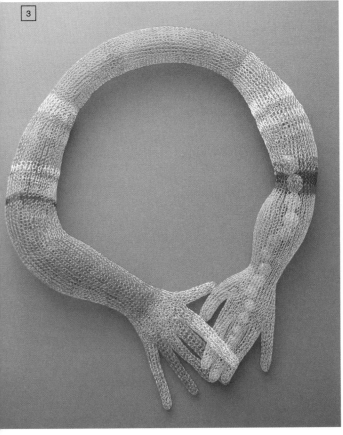

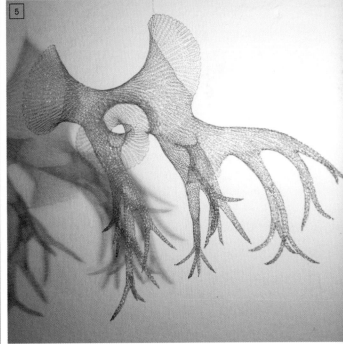

Cathrine Kullberg

NORWAY

No need to close our eyes and imagine light filtering between treetops to feel peaceful. We can keep them wide open and simply gaze at Cathrine Kullberg's creation *par excellence* – a lamp that exudes the calm of the forest glade. Cathrine was inspired by the classic Scandinavian tradition of using thin wood veneer strips for lighting. Her 'Norwegian Forest' lights display a pine grove, complete with animals, seen in light and shade. Famously, Scandinavian design tends to favour wood as a basic material for furnishings; Cathrine has gone one step further and opted for wood that can receive an extraordinary level of detail and complexity of design, courtesy of high-tech laser-cutting technology. Wood is a living material: it breathes, expands and contracts; it sweats

and dries. Cathrine loves the challenges it offers. 'Using particularly thin veneer is not the easiest choice,' she admits, 'but it is rewarding to work with a delicate and ever-changing material. Not one piece of wood is the same, exactly like us human beings.' She likes to use Swedish birch veneer for its lovely translucency, as well as its ability to be laser-cut, since its millimetre-thin, fragile surface has to be forced into a drum shape and given three-dimensional expression. Of her early trials, Cathrine confesses, 'An untouched sheet of veneer is holy, somehow, at least in the almost pristine Scandinavian aesthetic tradition, and I experienced a childish amusement by slicing it.' Her cuts had to be mostly diagonal, otherwise the veneer sheet would crack. Nowadays the veneer is carefully laser-cut by a skilled airplane model-maker. The steel frames for the lamps are custom-made at a metal workshop and powder-coated white. The finished items are then assembled by hand in Cathrine's Oslo studio. For table lights, thin natural leather lace is twined around the legs to soften the friction against the surface, then the shell is hand-sewn onto the frame using the same leather lace. For Cathrine, her craft is natural in every sense. 'The veneer sheet is simply begging to become a lamp,' she laughs. 'It softens stricter, modernistic interiors and the warmth of the material creates a friendly atmosphere. I think people enjoy the comfort provided by an authentic appearance and a warm light.' When lit, the blond birch veneer gives out a magical glow, and the delicately cut forest and eagle motifs allow white light to filter gently between the highlights of the trees. Sigh...

See also p. 284
www.cathrinekullberg.com

1

1 The splendour of the Norwegian forest experience is enhanced by the warm glow filtering through the cut-out natural birch veneer.

2 A glimpse inside Cathrine Kullberg's tool box.

3 Preparing a newly cut-out birch veneer sheet for folding around a metal frame to result in the 'Norwegian Forest' table lamp.

4 The 'Norwegian Forest' large pendant light in white stained ash is a superb sculptural centrepiece above a festive dining table.

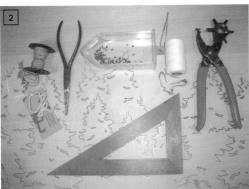

Cecilia Levy

SWEDEN

If you ever board a train in the countryside near Stockholm, you may bump into Cecilia Levy and possibly interrupt her seeking inspiration. She says, 'Travelling by train is so relaxing. I find it the ultimate place for thinking and reflecting about ideas.' Cecilia was born in Sweden, but actually grew up in three very different locations: a gated community in Kentucky, the bustling, hot city of Jakarta, and the family home in a rural suburb of Stockholm. Every time she moved, she had to assimilate all over again. This early exposure to travel and life abroad forged her ability to adapt. 'I am a rootless and restless person, who loves to be at home, wherever that is,' she confides. Of her precocious creativity, she says, 'I have always known I wanted to work with my hands.' Experience in graphic design and bookbinding contributed to give her an expertise with illustration and paper, but also reinforced her wish to explore a more tactile and immediate form of craft. Through her projects Cecilia challenges the fragility of paper, reinvents its surface with naturalistic and evocative drawings, and experiments with various coatings

and ingredients. 'When visiting antiquarians or second-hand bookshops,' she explains, 'I pick out books to my liking by the quality of the paper inside. The title is important, but it's not what catches my eye first.' She enthuses about second-hand books and packaging materials; paper with a history or a purpose, with visible wear and tear, and the marks of time. Cecilia works from home and shares a studio with her husband, illustrator Mattias Adolfsson. A member of Svenska Tecknare (the Association of Swedish Illustrators and Graphic Designers), she makes her delicate goods – whether functional or decorative – by hand. She also does work to commission, mostly in graphic design. Last but not least, she creates and exhibits art pieces. Drawing, or leaving a mark, is her passion. Paper is her material of choice, whether it holds the crispness of the new or the comfort and mystery of the old. Either way, she creates work that is nothing less than extraordinary.

See also p. 294
www.cecilialevy.com

1 Cecilia Levy organizing pre-cut paper strips on her work-table.

2 The paper strips are dipped into a freshly prepared glue mix before being adhered to a mould.

3 The decorative 'Petal' bowl consists of scalloped paper strips, carefully layered and glued together.

4 Cecilia's traditional tool set contains everything she needs to cut, slice, measure, stitch, and much more.

Cecilia Levy

5 The spine of the book 'Travels Without Destiny' is ingeniously made out of a slender tree branch.

6 The book should remain open so the reader can cherish its folded centre page, tree-stump illustrations and swirling hand-stitching.

7 This book jacket is adorned with an intricate botanical illustration and delicate stitching.

8 Stains have never looked so beautiful: this 'Coffee Constellations' artwork is a book page that has been stained with coffee and drawn onto with geometric, gem-like patterns.

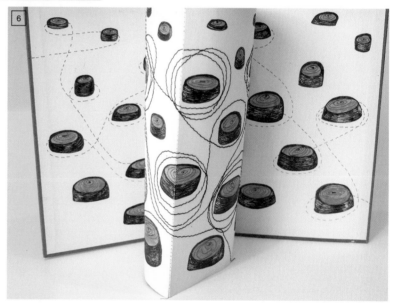

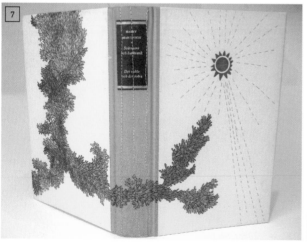

9 The fragile and poetic
'Live Happily Ever After'
cup is a feat of papier-mâché
craftsmanship.

Chizu Kobayashi

ITALY

'When I was younger, everything in my house signalled an opportunity to play and create. Plastic bottles, food packaging, wrapping paper, strings and buttons ... all these bits and pieces were my toys, not dolls,' recalls Niigata-born Chizu Kobayashi. From a young age she could be found cutting, sewing, pasting, painting, building little houses with furniture, and creating home and fashion accessories and other small objects. She spent a few years in the United States when still young, and remembers her emotional reaction on first seeing the work of Alexander Calder at the Whitney Museum. She was both impressed and touched by the humour and the love shown in his creations, and these factors doubtless had an influence on her work to come. Her first wire sculpture was a small torso covered with Japanese paper, inspired by Jean Paul Gaultier's famous perfume bottle. It is no surprise that Chizu majored in metalcraft at Musashino Art University in Tokyo. After a few years spent working as a freelance publicist, she decided to move to Bologna, Italy, and to become an artist. Not having special metalworking tools with her for brazing or welding, she naturally went back to wirework. She starts simply by 'sketching in the air' with a wire. Consequently, her creations end up looking like three-dimensional drawings. 'I love working with wire,' she says, 'because, even if you create a big object, the structure is so light that it doesn't feel as if it occupies the space, plus it projects shadows on the wall; interesting special effects.' The enormous flexibility offered by wirework allows Chizu to create chimerical and humorous objects, such as animals cut in half and displayed on either side of a wall. 'The traditional Japanese clean and refined lines of *ukiyoe*, literally "floating world", have definitely influenced me. The way I choose the lines, the lightness, the effect of the light and shade, is what makes my art quintessentially Japanese,' Chizu declares. That and the way in which she wraps her creations – an elaborate origami style. 'My sources of inspiration are above all in nature,' she says. 'Shadows of leaves against a wall, reflections on the water, colours of the clouds, odour of the grass in the early morning: nature offers us plenty of little happy moments, and it is my biggest joy to channel these in my craft.' Mission accomplished. Chizu's wired creatures put smiles on our faces and poetry back in our lives.

See also p. 290
www.chizkobject.com

1 Orderly, simple and fresh, Chizu Kobayashi's workshop shelves reflect her light artistry.

2 Equipped with small pliers, Chizu finishes some knotting on one of her extraordinary sculptures.

3 An origami paper construction wraps around the 'Rabbit Cage': add fine cord and a company card, and you have the most ravishing gift.

4 Charm and wit found in the everyday, or how to spot the intruder: a lemon with metal bunny ears has wormed its way into a line-up of figs.

Chizu Kobayashi

5 Who thought only ghosts could do this? A powerful stallion, 'Black Beauty', passes through the wall in a feat of wire magic.

6 'Birds', a whimsically poetic tealight-holder set.

7 You will go to the ball, thanks to this pretty 'Ballerina' wire creation.

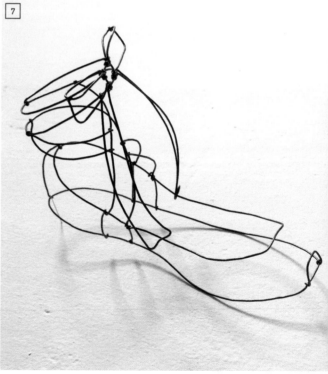

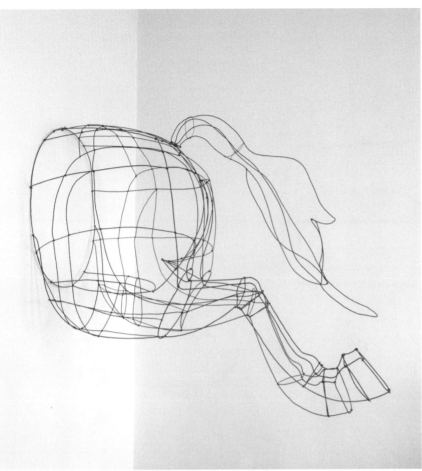

8

8 Wired together for life,
happily ever after: Chizu's
'Just Married' wire sculpture.

9 Chizu's home is adorned
with her wire decorations,
including the grapevine wall
fixture and the humorous
'Beastie' fruit baskets under
one of her paintings.

Claire Coles
UK

The ultimate luxury in craft and applied arts for a 'home sweet home'; a one-of-a-kind, beautifully embroidered, creatively reinterpreted ornament for a wall. We are talking about a bespoke wallpaper by Claire Coles. Her couture wallcoverings transcend the basic function of wallpaper, in that they literally transform walls into unique, large-scale works of art. From her studio in London, Claire takes fragments of vintage wallpapers and manipulates them with silk and leather, playing with both texture and scale. She sources her vintage papers, ranging from acid flocks to blowsy florals, from markets and charity shops. The delicate and skilled process she follows involves cutting, layering and then machine-stitching papers together to create a rich assemblage of panoramas and images. Her layering and intricate embroidery form an exquisite and detailed work of art that appeals not only to the eye but also to the touch. The wallpapers are tactile because each surface presents a delicate texture, that of the threads running through them, like veins under a vellum skin. Claire has a predilection for flora and fauna, and for bird patterns in particular – a vast source of inspiration that allows her designs to grow, come to life and creep across walls, lending a romantic and ethereal quality to a room. All of her wallpapers are handcrafted in the studio, made to order and designed specifically according to the client's space, whether private or commercial (Claire has collaborated with, among others, renowned boutiques and distinguished department stores). Alongside her wallpaper collection, she designs artworks for the gift market, and she also sells gift items including stationery, ceramics and decorative objects through her online shop. Her work is a great representation of what modern artisanship can be: meticulously conceived and made, traditional yet unmistakably contemporary, intrinsic to the style and culture of its national heritage. In Claire's case, it is almost hybrid; a unique theatrical luxury.

See also pp. 274, 299, 304
www.clairecolesdesign.co.uk

1 Claire Coles firmly guides a wallpaper panel through her sewing machine in order to create the desired pattern.

2 A finished roll of 'Garden' wallpaper with exquisite floral collages and embroideries.

3 Vintage wallpapers, cards, cups and artworks all live together in Claire's vibrant studio.

2

3

4 The 'Midnight Garden' one-off wallcovering showcases giant flowers for an instant romantic setting.

5 The 'Paris' one-off wallcovering transforms any room into a cosy boudoir inspired by the City of Lights.

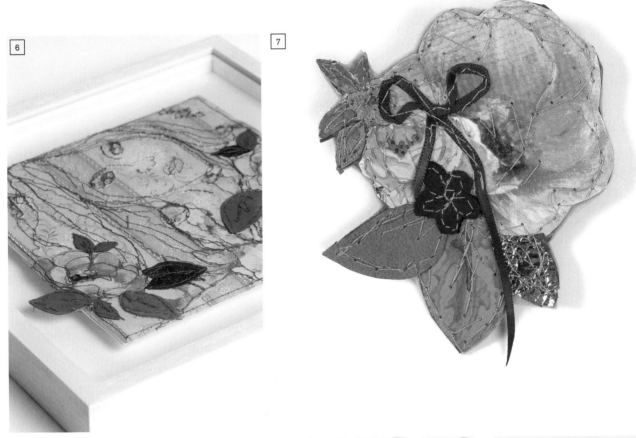

6 A framed, delicately
embroidered picture from
the 'Girls' series.

7 The 'Wallpaper' brooch will
enhance a corsage or lapel,
unless it is simply cherished
as art on a wall.

8 Each mug is printed with
Claire's trademark stitched
designs, offering a delightful
trompe-l'œil surface.

Cynthia Vardhan

USA

When Cynthia Vardhan was 13 years old, she enrolled in an after-school pottery class at the recreational centre in her hometown of Roanoke, Virginia. At 15, her parents were kind enough to buy her her own pottery wheel. At 17, she selected her college based solely on its ceramics studio. Although she took a degree in linguistics, she spent every waking moment in the ceramics building and knew all along that she wanted to become a ceramic designer. This field, however, does not offer an obvious career path in the US, so Cynthia tried to direct her own ceramic design education by splitting time between the ceramics department and the industrial design department of the MFA Rochester Institute of Technology. She went on to work at Columbus College of Art & Design, while building up her studio and becoming a full-time designer/artist/craftsman. Her studio takes up the entire third floor of her house in downtown Columbus, Ohio. It is up in the treetops, with a splendid view, and it contains everything a potter could dream of: wheel, kiln, mixer, sink, glaze room, dry materials, storage, work-tables…

'My inspiration is precious,' confides Cynthia, and so she confines intriguing source material to 'the one clean part of the studio and the office; there I have pictures around the mirror and above the sink, as well as all my sketchbooks, maps, photo albums and ephemera that I've picked up and filed away for future use'. Subjects that capture Cynthia's imagination include aerial photography, ancient maps, roads, brickwork, stone walls, old Islamic/ Middle Eastern ceramics, Japanese textile design, Mughal miniatures, Italian Renaissance maiolica, Indian henna, royal Thai textiles and paisleys. As can be deduced, travel is a vital part of Cynthia's artistic life. Indeed, her work can be thought of as a history of her travels and the environments in which she has found herself. Her 'Geography' pieces are like postcards tracking the connections between a person, their memories and locations significant to them. Her 'Commemoration' plates are like snapshots that capture suburban America, and her functional pieces bear patterns that are collages of traditional decorations gathered from many sources. 'My relationship to ceramics has become marital. There are so many things about it that are irritating but I love it, I am devoted to it, and it's never ever dull,' declares Cynthia, with sparkles in her eyes.

See also p. 256
www.cynthiavardhan.com

1 'Summer Grove', part of Cynthia Vardhan's 'Commemoration' series: the nostalgic beauty of suburban America captured in a fine piece of porcelain decorated with iron and slip decals.

2 Cynthia delicately slip-trailing a decorated vessel.

3 The 'Geography' series reinterprets stoneware and slip vessels as postcards or snapshots of memories of certain locations. 'I would like to go home now', shown here, displays a specific urban mapping.

4 Views from above: fields and details from maps are captured forever in 'Weather is here, wish you were nice' stoneware and slip from the 'Geography' series.

1

2

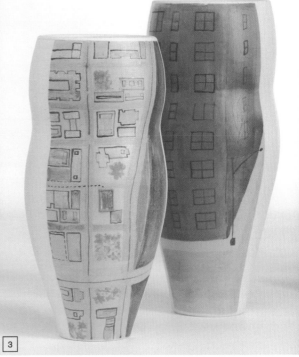

3

4

Depeapa

SPAIN

The Spanish for 'from start to finish' is *de pe a pa*. In Veronica de Arriba's world, it is written 'Depeapa', and it has proved the perfect name for her new venture. Veronica has always been an obsessive illustrator. Even from childhood, she says, 'I drew endlessly. I wouldn't stop drawing dolls and offering them to my family.' One sunny day in late 2007, as she was wandering for inspiration around the city of Granada, where she lives, she spontaneously wrote down 'de pe a pa', liked the sound of it and immediately knew that she would use it. By this time she had been working as a graphic designer and illustrator for several years, but now she had the idea that she could 'give a new life to my poetic illustrations by utilizing the original drawings to create accessories made out of wood, felt, cotton or paper: a start-to-finish handmade process'. At first she didn't intend to sell anything; this was simply a project of love. However, as soon as she posted images of her pieces on the internet, she began to receive enthusiastic requests from individuals and shops. This was the beginning of a small craft business. Inspired by various sources, including interior decor, photography, movies, books, travel, flowers, walking, people-watching and dreaming, Veronica draws melancholic and sensitive characters, animals and flowers, then finds the best way to fulfil each illustration's potential. Her naïve illustrations, with their thin lines and warm colours, might adorn hand-sewn, felt-detailed cameo brooches, or cut and sanded wooden accessories, or screenprinted cushions, or reversible resin necklaces with a drawing on each side. 'I love the thought of my characters travelling to different homes around the world and starting their new life there,' enthuses their creator. 'I especially get chills when I picture my brooches on people's lapels.' Veronica is a strong believer that one should do one's utmost to crack a smile from whomever one encounters during the day, be it with a quirky brooch of a moustachioed face or a pert rooster. 'What is a day without humour and whimsicality?' she asks. Surely it's a day without a Depeapa piece in sight.

See also pp. 249, 275, 307, 312
www.depeapa.com

1 If these walls could talk…
They can! Two chattering
illustrations from Depeapa's
'Conversation' series.

2 A delightful surprise:
colourful cameo brooches
featuring an array of neatly
dressed animals.

3 Highly representative of
Veronica de Arriba's drawing
style, this 'Niña' cotton
brooch is a sweet companion
for your lapel.

4 Veronica sewing a scalloped
ribbon around the edge of an
illustrated cotton brooch.

5 Buy a drawing … on wood: a series of adorable illustrated pendants.

6 Why would these 'Man' and 'Woman' cotton cushions be blushing? Love at first sight?

7 Veronica infuses tenderness and wit into every work she creates, including this handkerchief painted with a charming doe dressed to the nines.

8 'Collares ganchillo': fine crochet patterns in baby pink or blue for these pretty necklaces.

9 The kind of rainclouds that nobody minds: a pendant necklace with notebook scraps providing the pattern.

Duvelleroy
FRANCE

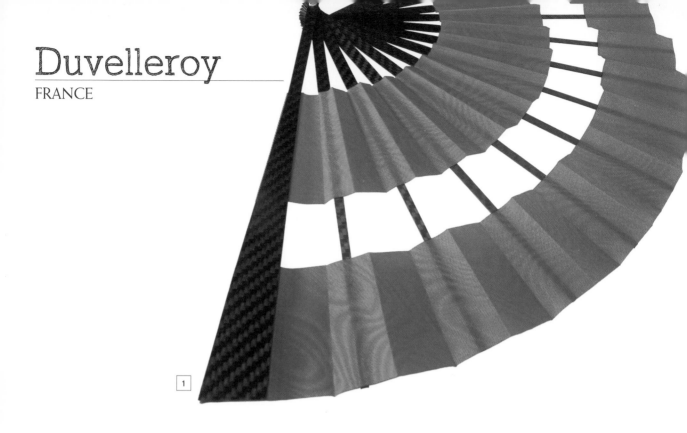

1

2

1 The watered silk leaf and carbon-fibre guards and sticks of the half-moon-shaped 'Cabriolet' fan offer an incomparable lightness.

2 Illuminate your nights with the warm glow of the 'Winter Sun' fan, made of silk organza painted with gold, copper and silver flakes, with carbon-fibre guards and sticks.

3 Pleating is done in a fast and precise gesture: the symmetry has to be perfect.

4 Luxurious packaging for a precious companion.

5 The *ennoblement* of the leaf is accomplished by craftsmen who patiently apply paint and lace, and embroider the finest sequins.

Duvelleroy is the only Parisian house of fans that has survived to the present day. In 2010, Eloïse Gilles and Raphäelle de Panafieu joined in partnership with the firm's last heir in a venture to resurrect the house and secure its place in the contemporary fashion world. The company was originally founded in 1827 by Jean-Pierre Duvelleroy, and its delicately crafted fans rapidly became the sought-after pinnacle of the French fan-making style. As official supplier to royalty, starting with Queen Victoria, the company also created the fans given to statesmen's spouses for their official engagements in France. During the nineteenth century, the firm published *The Language of the Fan*, a small booklet explaining the coded gestures used by women to communicate messages such as 'I am engaged', 'Follow me' and 'Do you love me?' Although the tradition of using fans declined in the West, Duvelleroy's descendant conserved vintage fans, moulds and sketches, contributing to an exhibition on fans at the Galliera Museum in Paris. He kept alive the dream that the company would one day shine again. That day dawned when Eloïse and Raphäelle appeared. Duvelleroy luxury folding fans are now fashioned, using techniques that are faithful to the tradition of French fan-making, by couture designers. Their manufacture combines the know-how of a dozen specialist artisans, including sculptors, engravers and embroiderers. Each fan starts with an idea – something for a bride, for the night, for the day – and finds its equilibrium in the harmony between the outer guards, inner sticks and pleated leaf. Raw precious materials such as horn, ebony and mother-of-pearl are sliced to obtain wafer-thin sticks only nine-tenths of a millimetre thick. These are shaped into frames. 'The losses are significant, but this is necessary to obtain frames that lose nothing of their lightness,' explain Eloïse and Raphäelle. Next, organza, silk, muslin and lace are pleated in a mould, following a two-hundred-year-old technique. The leaf's *ennoblement* is the charge of gold-fingered craftsmen, who patiently apply paint and embroider sequins with the finest of threads. Only one of the last fan-makers in France has the mastery to accomplish the final stage of mounting the leaves by hand, in the purest French tradition. Once assembled, the leaf is hand-trimmed. The rivet at the base of the fan is stamped with a golden daisy, Duvelleroy's emblem, dating back to the Art Nouveau period. All is realized in the name of the 'beauty of the gesture'.

See also p. 315
www.duvelleroy.fr

6

7

6 Exceptional glamour: the leaves of the lavish 'Midnight Bird' are comprised of eighteen blue ostrich feathers and an intricate origami of silk muslin.

7 The sumptuous design of the 'Midnight Bird' is completed by guards and sticks in natural green mother-of-pearl.

8 Dazzle your audience by parading the 'Gust of Wind', whose emerald satin-silk leaf, embellished with gold flakes, is a spell in itself. The guards and sticks are of polished horn.

9 A spectacular sight despite its practical compact size, the 'Coral Galalith' has a leaf made of coral satin silk, with guards and sticks in galalith imitating tortoiseshell.

8

9

Eileen Gatt

UK

Enter the mesmerizing, mythical universe of Scottish silversmith Eileen Gatt, who, with an element of fantasy, brings ancient legends into the contemporary world. After graduating from the Royal College of Art in London, Eileen returned home to the Highlands to set up her jewelry and silversmithing business in the Black Isle. This beautiful peninsula provides her with the perfect working environment, especially as she has long been fascinated by the mystical interaction between man and sea. Eileen was given a Creative Development Award by the Scottish Arts Council to produce a collection of work inspired by Scottish folklore. She collaborated with three Highland storytellers and used their tales, together with other Scottish customs, to inspire new designs. She likes to use tales and customs as a starting point, creating her own visual interpretations and abstracting them in such a way that the pieces convey an air of mystery and intrigue. A number of her recent creations incorporate elements that have been cast from rowan trees. Rowan was believed to protect people from the *sidh* (the wee folk or

fairies), so is a symbol of good luck. The hare – an animal associated with superstition and myth – is also prevalent in Eileen's work. People once believed that witches could transform themselves into hares and therefore the animals were often feared, though conversely they were also symbolic of fertility and thus considered to be lucky. Eileen also makes references to seals, known as selkies in Scottish folklore. Tales of people who could turn into seals and live under the sea as well as on land were very common around the shores of the Black Isle, as they were throughout Scotland. Eileen's magical collections include one-off commissioned items and pieces for exhibition; she also makes gifts for children, such as cups, spoons and charm bracelets. She works predominantly in silver, but often incorporates 18-carat gold and semi-precious stones to highlight aspects of the design, thereby creating an enthralling treasure trove to be cherished for years to come.

See also pp. 282, 293
www.eileengatt.co.uk

1 Soldering charms onto the chain of a bracelet with the aid of a blowtorch.

2 Precious little animals in 18-carat gold, looking as if they are about to dive into the inviting depths of their silver vessels.

3 A lively collection of 'Amulet Rowan Twig' brooches form a mythical wonderland of silver, 18-carat gold and resin.

4 'Amulet Pebble' brooches in silver, 18-carat gold and resin reflect Scottish legends in which animals carry magical significance.

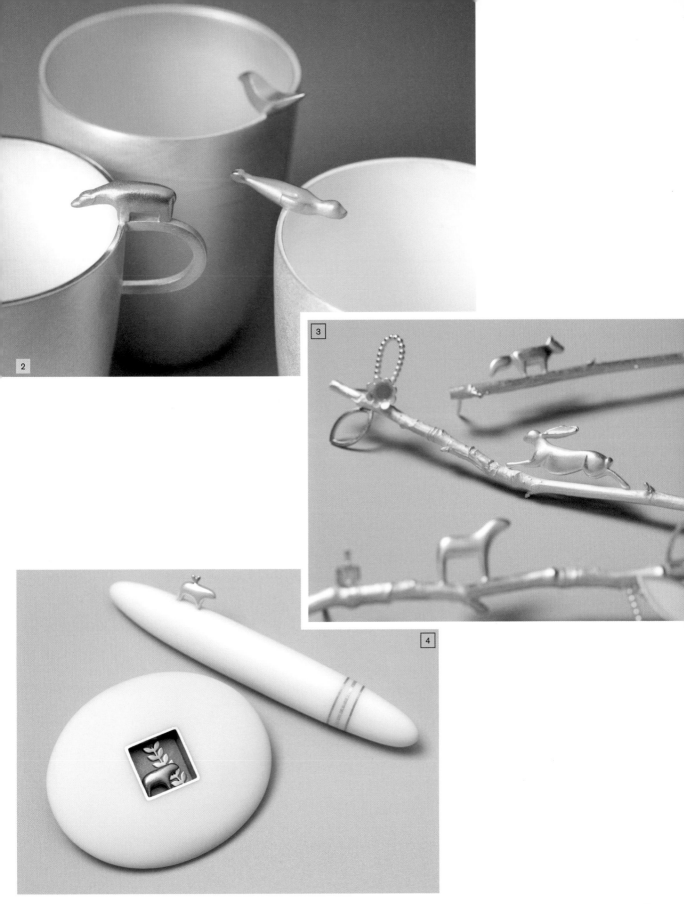

Elisa Strozyk

GERMANY

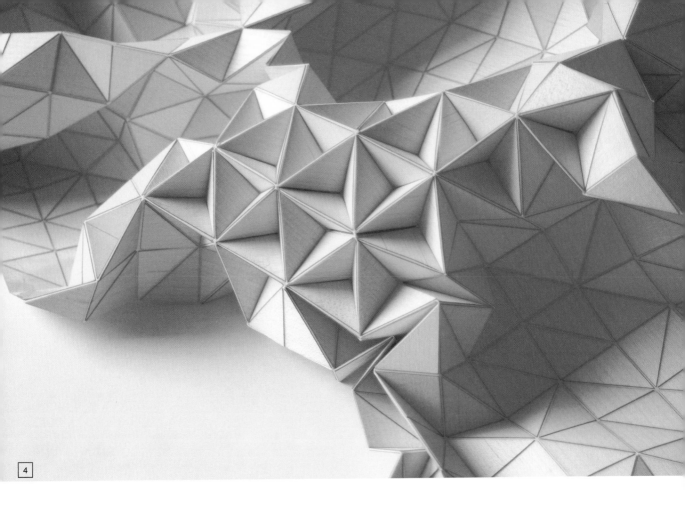

4

1 Elisa Strozyk weaving the textile background onto which her wood veneer leftovers will be attached.

2 The finely cut triangular veneer pieces form a pleasing regular pattern once assembled on the textile surface.

3 Elisa's compact studio allows her easy access to the various components required for her meticulous work.

4 The finished textiles are highly flexible and can be morphed into a multitude of shapes.

We are used to experiencing wood as a hard material – we know the feeling of walking across a wooden floor, or touching the bark of a tree – but 'Wooden Textiles' offer a whole new tactile experience. German textile designer Elisa Strozyk has been researching ways of interweaving wood with textiles to make it flexible and soft. The outcome is a hybrid matter that is half wood/half textile, somewhere between hard and soft, challenging all our perceptions. It looks and smells familiar but it surprises us, as it is able to move in unexpected ways. It is so innovative that Elisa was recently awarded the Young Designer's Prize at the German Design Awards. 'The world around us is becoming increasingly immaterial,' she states, 'and highlighting surfaces that are desirable to touch can reconnect us with the material world and enhance the emotional value of the object.' The process of creating a flexible wooden surface involves deconstructing wood veneer leftovers into smaller pieces, which are then attached to a textile base. The material is cut into tiles, and these are stuck together by hand to form a textile-like surface. The flexibility of the textile is dependent upon the geometric shape of the tiles and the size of the gaps between them. A triangular shape affords the best ability to move, the isosceles triangle being the most versatile. A pattern of uneven triangles of various sizes performs more unpredictable movements. 'Wooden Textiles' is an approach to responsible thinking about products, their lifecycle and their sustainability. For Elisa this means 'utilizing materials that are able to grow old beautifully, while working with recycled objects and material waste'. She has applied 'Wooden Textiles' to everyday life, be it with her highly flexible carpet that can be rolled up, laid flat or sculptured in dramatic ways, or with her unconventional 'Miss Maple' pendant light, a cross between a sculptural object and a functional decorative lamp, whose surface is broken down into a grid of triangles that allow the lampshade to be transformed manually in three-dimensional ways. 'It is crucial to aim for a closer relationship between subject and object,' says Elisa. Thanks to her, objects of the future will challenge us and provide an open invitation to reconnect with what we find around us.

See also pp. 287, 309
www.elisastrozyk.de

Esque Studio

USA

Experimenting with form and technique is paramount to Esque's core ambition. This glass design and blowing studio, founded by Justin Parker and Andi Kovel, pays an extraordinary attention to detail and quality to achieve a coherent vision of functional accessories, lighting and architectural elements. Justin and Andi, driven by an interest in the inherent attributes of glass, infuse their knowledge into the design of each piece, so that it becomes both a fine piece of art and a sought-after collectible of the future. Adding to its value, each piece is unique and handmade to order. The work also benefits from Esque's state-of-the art 'eco mission'. Their studio was built using cutting-edge technology to reduce waste and gas consumption. Two wind-powered furnaces run up to ten times more efficiently than traditional gas furnaces and produce zero CO_2 emissions. Approximately 100 pounds of glass waste is recycled weekly into the smaller of the two furnaces and then re-used to produce eco-products, 100% recycled and chemical-free. Justin and Andi started as glass blowers for hire and found that time 'linked us together as far as our passion for, and interest in, pushing the medium goes. We are each other's perfect foil.' The duo have risen to international acclaim over the past ten years (they were recently honoured by *Time* magazine as one of the 'Design 100', today's one hundred most influential international designers) and now lead the American market for hand-blown, modern, functional glasswork. Justin, most famous for his skill in creating enormous pieces of glass, studied under Italian masters with a focus on handmade glass sculpture. He is an accomplished artist, exhibiting at venues including the Brooklyn Museum of Art, and he has also produced fine art pieces for artists including Jim Dine, Kiki Smith and Tony Oursler. Andi, meanwhile, is internationally celebrated as an influential accessory designer, glass blower and fine artist. She has exhibited with Claes Oldenburg, Damien Hirst and Kiki Smith, and has designed glass lines for Ralph Lauren and Donna Karan, but she is most recognized for her new forms and techniques in the field of glass. Such a combination of talent in such a specialty field could only produce a collection of gorgeous vessels and edgy decorative accessories: a feast for the eye and a prize for the home.

See also pp. 270, 287
www.esque-studio.com

1 'Knoll' vases, with their delicious citrus-y colour scheme – persimmon, pink, orange and beige – and their generous lumpy form.

2 Andi Kovel papering a newly blown piece in order to perfect its shape.

3 Justin Parker blowing a large, almost perfect glass bubble, in Esque Studio's vast workshop.

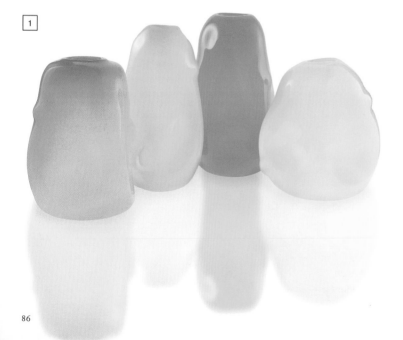

5

4 An assortment of brown
iridescent glass bottles neatly
aligned in 'JP's Apothecary'.

5 'Animated Bookends' make
for a humorous way to
display one's books.

6 'Hands up!' one might
exclaim when holding this
lustrous gold '.38 Special'
glass paperweight.

6

Fric de Mentol

PORTUGAL

Innocent, fun, refreshing, colourful, playful, often ebullient and whimsical: works by Portuguese artist Ana Raimundo are deeply embedded in her country's folk traditions and comprise a fine balance of past archetypes mixed with modern references. 'Each subject present in my creative sphere is based on the Portuguese culture and my personal take on it,' says Ana, a freelance artist, who very early on developed a fondness for sketching the world around her. Her first works adorned the walls of her family home, but she was soon tempted to use markers on paper, opening up further opportunities to express herself artistically. A few years later, by now interested in fashion models, she started drawing stylish clothing for women of different body types, creating a collection for real women in sharp contrast to the diktats of high fashion. She then began to explore abstract painting on canvas, and, after a few successful exhibitions, enrolled in art college so as to enrich and perfect her natural creative instincts by the study of human relations and expressions. She still favoured painting on canvas, but started exploring other areas such as tile painting.

This immersion in a period of discovery, and absorption of newfound knowledge, allowed her to embrace her native culture, and she began to win awards in the competitions she entered. After a few years working for a Portuguese company specializing in tile painting, she heard the voice of freedom calling and embarked on the project of running her own business. Fric de Mentol was born as an online venture. 'The internet brought a new modern significance to my activity, but I have always preferred the old ways,' confides Ana. 'This is reflected in the handmade process that all my objects go through.' Her creations soon became smaller, so that people could carry them around, and they evolved towards the concept of wearable art. But, whether endearing illustration or stationery, pretty screenprinted lavender bag or quirky little badge, Ana's entire collection is expressive and personal, filled with vitality and charm; a cut above the 'craft' norm, thanks to her complete and passionate artistic involvement.

See also pp. 275, 299, 309
http://dropesdementol.blogspot.com

1 Ana Raimundo's invigorating
workshop, with its works
in progress, inspirational
images and tools of all sorts:
a multitasker's creative den.

2 The lavender bag production
line: screenprinted cotton
panels, threads and lavender
seeds sit neatly side by side.

3 A sensitive painter, Ana
has the gift of capturing
human expressions, as in
'Loneliness', a touching
portrait of a young girl
with haunting eyes.

4 Textile bunting, colourful
illustrations and vivid
paintings attest to Ana's
wide creative range.

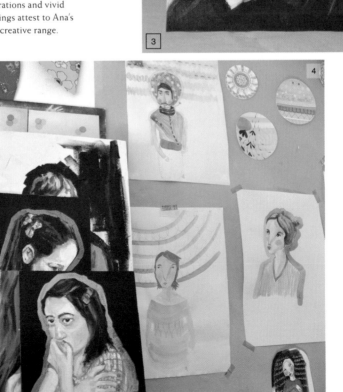

5 Clay brooch panels are progressively finely painted so that each ends up unique.

6 *'Bom dia!'* seem to exclaim these delightful clay brooches, whose characters sport kaleidoscopic beanies.

7 Ana's graphic style is exemplified in this figurative brooch: a balanced use of vibrant colour and a naïve yet non-caricatured portrayal.

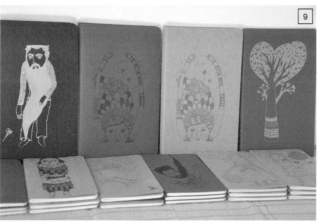

8 It's party time: wear a bubbly hand-stitched pin, and spin!

9 A collection of notebooks whose covers have been screenprinted with reinterpretations of traditional Portuguese characters.

10 The 'Lollipop Girl' is one of Ana's trademark figures, seen here on notebook covers.

Furor Brillante
FRANCE

Botanicals, especially flowers, and more importantly the organic world, are a major influence for virtuoso embroiderer Andréas Kanellopoulos. His often vivid raw materials – precious beads and sequins, spools of silk thread, sumptuous ribbons – are the guiding forces that inspire and direct his hands, which work without a pattern. Thanks to the glorious colours and textures of his components, Andréas is able to experiment with a multitude of combinations, which – often seemingly by accident – result in spectacular creations. Born in Athens but now based in Paris, Andréas studied academic and technical drawing, art history and theatre. He became a costumier, designing costumes for the theatre and opera in France and overseas. At the same time he started studying *broderie d'art* (art embroidery), which led to the creation of a jewelry and accessory collection. He also worked to commission, producing special-occasion items, such as embroidered clothing for children. Soon he was working exclusively in art embroidery and textile embellishment, particularly for haute couture and luxury ready-to-wear, and Furor Brillante ('a furor that shines') was launched, offering both traditional and contemporary adornments. Of the two main tools that Andréas utilizes – a Luneville crochet hook and a needle – he prefers the needle, as this allows him more freedom. He is also keen on any additional application that can help him transform his raw materials to obtain effects of volume and avant-garde texture. 'I burn, I fray, I rip, I cut and distort,' he exclaims. 'My passion for embroidery totally resonates with my love of historical costumes and haute couture. Working in the luxury artisan trade and promoting its inherent values – excellence, and perpetuating tradition and knowledge – gives me pleasure, and is also my way of opposing the excessive standardization and dehumanization of our world.' In a society that fiercely resists all traces of time, Furor Brillante's embroideries are an anchor. The sparkling evidence of Andréas's emotions and presence are left on the fabric. 'Time is my accomplice,' he muses, 'and it helps confer symbolic value on my work.' His only ambition is to continue on his journey, perhaps diversifying into other disciplines that share the same philosophy. 'I wish my creations could exist not only in their current form – garments – but also in other fields, such as furnishings and interior design.' Ferociously brilliant indeed!

See also p. 314
http://furorbrillante.blogspot.com

1 Andréas Kanellopoulos works with a vast colour spectrum, encompassing the subtlest variations of tone, as can be seen on his breathtaking shelves of silk threads.

2 Exquisite embroidery on pale pink satin silk, with metallic sequins, multicoloured Lurex threads, Bohemian crystal glass, silk tape and tubular glass beads.

3 Spectacular embroidery on lilac jacquard cotton, with applied ribbons, satin and cup sequins, and tubular glass and satin beads.

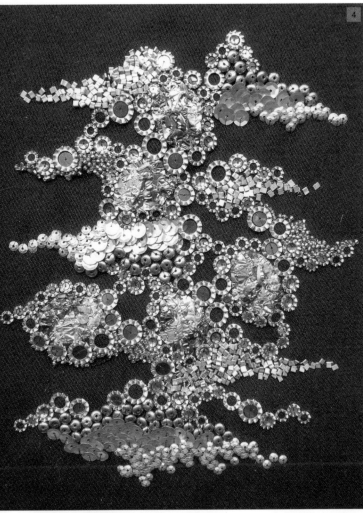

4 Glamorous embroidery
on black woollen grain de
poudre, with lacy golden
sequins, flattened and
crushed paper elements,
cup sequins and tubular
thin-metal beads.

5 Andréas at work on his
traditional embroidery frame.

6 The stylish card conveys the
excellence of Andréas's craft.

7 A seamstress's dummy
draped with a ravishing
floral embroidery tester
against the striking
showstopper of a black-
and-white inspiration wall.

8 Pulchritudinous embroidery
on fuchsia satin silk,
with vintage trimmings,
nineteenth-century buttons,
silk tape, cup sequins, Lurex
thread, rhinestones and jet
beads.

8

Géraldine Gonzalez

FRANCE

A graduate of the textile department at the Duperré School of Applied Arts in Paris, Géraldine Gonzalez first worked as a shoe designer, but she has now made her name as an extraordinary sculptor of paper. Her work has been used in advertising, in the media and in children's books, and has also been exhibited in individual and group shows at such well-known venues as the Grand Palais and the Centre Pompidou in Paris. Today, however, her focus is on flamboyant, made-to-order interior and window decorations. She has experimented with all manner of materials, including papier-mâché, cloth, crushed glass and pearls, but has now found her favourite – 'the prince, crystal paper, a material with a lovely name', which allows her 'delicately to play with transparency and light'. Using this precious paper, Géraldine crafts figurine lamps, iguanas, chrysalides and ant skeletons, Chinese votives and exquisite fashion accessories (lingerie, hats, gloves, shoes), all of which have been displayed in upscale department stores and shops such as Le Bon Marché and the Printemps Haussmann in Paris,

Mint and Liberty in London, and the John Derian Company in New York. The list of her devoted followers is impressive: she has worked with many luxury houses, including Christian Lacroix, Sonia Rykiel, Chantal Thomass, Baccarat, Van Cleef & Arpels, Givenchy and Kenzo. Her resumé includes the creation of special Christmas windows for the launches of 'La Petite Robe Noire' fragrance and the 'Abeille Royale' range for French luxury house Guerlain, and also the crafting of 'Médusas', huge sparkly crystal jellyfish sculptures, for the Merano Palace Hotel in Italy. Recent works – 'imprints of mystery and fragility' – look as if they have come from an enchanted forest. Géraldine has created 'a giant tree house, shimmering amulets, burning bushes, bearers of charms and spells, and a score of other living, curious – and magic – plant creatures'. She is an architect of fantastical scenes and celestial still lifes. Paper triumphs as a source of awe in her magnificent golden hands.

See also pp. 251, 285, 295
www.geraldinegonzalez.com

1 Géraldine Gonzalez uses a cardboard pattern to help her make final adjustments to a glorious papier-mâché dress.

2 A window display for Japanese shop Galerie Vie, with dresses floating so gently that it is hard to imagine they are made of hardened paper.

3 Fatal attraction: the heads of Printemps Haussmann department store window dummies were replaced with spectacular papier-mâché flowers for *Beauté Rare*, a men's fashion exhibition.

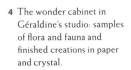

Géraldine Gonzalez

4 The wonder cabinet in Géraldine's studio: samples of flora and fauna and finished creations in paper and crystal.

5 Beauty is where you find it, a notion highly relevant to Géraldine's craft: this crystal skull is an extraordinary example.

6 A papier-mâché flower and spider detail from one of Géraldine's window displays.

7 A touch of grace: a paper and crystal butterfly.

8 Géraldine's workshop is a fascinating cabinet of curiosities, with sumptuous yet bizarre treasures, such as this little bird sculpted in paper and crystal.

101

Hanna af Ekström
SWEDEN

1

2

3

4

1 'Yours Sincerely, Aubrey
Beardsley' necklace, a
strong talismanic piece with
ropework attesting to Hanna
af Ekström's dexterity.

2 Chained up: a radiant blue
agate pendant necklace.

3 Hanna sawing out a piece of
jewelry from a sheet of steel,
a task that requires strength
and focus.

4 A box of Hanna's favourite
materials: gemstones (here,
coral), steel chains, ropes and
satin swatches.

Dark fairytales, antique treasures and the deep blue
sea form the core of Swedish designer Hanna af
Ekström's creative source material. Hanna collects
stuffed animals, shells, skulls and bones, and loves
to wander around the rooms of her local natural
history museum, delving into secret drawers and
rummaging on shelves. She gathers objects and
images of her ephemera onto moodboards that help
her visualize what art she might create. Naturally
her studio is located near the sea, in the heart of
Gothenburg, where she can look out at the big
harbour cranes from her window. She grew up on
an island in the northern archipelago and much
of her vision for making meaningful contemporary
jewelry comes from her upbringing. She took a
bachelor's degree in jewelry art, but then a master's
degree in graphic design. This dual education has
been a great asset, since both areas feed each
other perfectly. Hanna's jewelry collection contains
hidden stories and symbols that are up to the
wearer to interpret. She carefully includes black
hues and nuances, so that each piece has a strong
graphic impact against skin or clothing. She also
uses non-precious materials. What is represented
is more important than what it is represented by.
All of her jewelry is made by hand: some pieces

are carefully constructed in steel and burned black
with linseed oil, whereas textile works are made of
lengths of sailing rope stitched together. Generally
Hanna does not produce seasonal collections;
rather, she develops her jewelry line as it comes
to mind. She is keen to make a statement against
overconsumption, but she is also keen to preserve
quality and tradition. 'Lately I've been interested
in and inspired by clichés and misconceptions
about the New Age movement. By re-making
occult symbols and using sacred stones from the
Himalayas, I want to explore the question of origin
and belonging,' she says. 'How close can the
fashion world and the New Age movement come to
one another? What do they have in common, and
how can they interact?' Hanna's jewelry certainly
has a potent gothic vibe, a talismanic quality that
gives a dose of self-confidence to anyone lucky
enough to wear it.

See also p. 281
www.hannaafekstrom.com

Ikuko Iwamoto
UK

Fasten your diving suit and make an appearance at a bizarre 'tea ceremony'. Here, delicate teapots, cups and vases – apparently remnants of a mysterious underwater kingdom – proudly display their textured surfaces. These utilitarian yet extravagant vessels, adorned with raised dots or spikes, seem to be distant relatives of the more familiar coral, sea urchin or anemone. Their creator, Japanese ceramicist Ikuko Iwamoto, showcases her admirable knowhow and creativity from a little workshop in London. There she handcrafts her porcelain containers, always keeping an eye on developments to make ceramic creation a more eco-friendly process. She envisages eventually splitting her time between the UK and Japan, and her Japanese heritage remains a vivid source of inspiration. She is notably inspired by the traditional concept of *wabi-sabi* – a celebration of the beauty of the imperfect, impermanent and incomplete. She is keen to explore and develop her practice, and, with the support of the UK Crafts Council and Crafts Central, she has been able to purchase a large kiln, which has helped her make sizeable pieces. She has also investigated ways of creating more affordable items so as to expand her range and appeal to a wider audience. One way has been to craft smaller items, such as ceramic brooches, like friendly creatures from the bottom of the ocean

that one can tame and treasure. Ikuko describes her work as 'a world of intricacy and detail, of mathematical pattern and organic chaos, of beauty and repulsion'. To look at her precious collection is to imagine that she has the uncanny ability to zoom in on a microscopic world and then report on it through her meticulous creations. The purity of her deceptively simple work is strengthened by the use of white, though this is sometimes punctuated with tiny dotted injections of colour that give a life-affirming quality to works such as the 'Nucleolus' range. Ikuko's ceramics have won several awards, including the Ceramic Review Prize for Innovation at Ceramic Art London. Her collection – whether her appealing round forms with soft alcoves, or her hostile-looking items with sharp, fine spikes protruding inwards and outwards – invites the viewer to embark on a tactile odyssey. One cannot fail to be won over by the pure aesthetic en route.

See also pp. 265, 301
www.ikukoi.co.uk

1 These gorgeously bulbous sea urchin containers with removable lids are an invitation to touch.

2 Brittle porcelain tentacles swirl around the smooth shape of a white 'Spiky' vase.

3 Ikuko Iwamoto pours liquid clay into a mould in front of the large window that illuminates her London studio.

4 Despite their hostile appearance, Ikuko's white 'Spikyspiky' bowls exude artistry.

JAMESPLUMB
UK

Artists James Russell and Hannah Plumb met in 1998 while studying sculpture at Wimbledon School of Art. On graduating, the couple had separate practices and it took a while for them to realize that their individual sensibilities would work well together. Under their new combined name, they launched their company with what is now one of their most recognizable products, the 'Sampson Dog Light'. 'We enjoy working under the one name, as it represents the single artistic voice of both of us,' they say. Hannah's signature is her ability to find empathy with and stories in old objects, while James enjoys unveiling the beauty in the everyday. Attracted to timeworn things, the pair love to rummage around car boot sales and flea markets. Most of the pieces they buy are old and battered, but the main thing is that they all have a story to tell. The couple buy many varied items and like to marry them together within one creation. Both say that their found objects are often meant to be together. 'Since we hoard a lot of things, we sometimes find a new piece that perfectly matches something that we've had for ages. It's exciting to find two objects that speak to each other, but it can't be forced.' The pieces have to form a new character as one, while still retaining their individual identities. It is a delicate balance of retaining the original and yet allowing the whole to become more than the sum of its parts. When exhibiting their collections, Hannah and James create unique installations that are highly inspirational, a vision of nostalgia and beauty. No wonder that numerous retailers have called for their artistic input in designing interiors and windows. 'It's very important for us to present experiences for people and not just finished pieces. Our exhibitions have an experiential element for the viewer, and we love to bring the approach of an art installation to our interiors.' The couple work from home, an appealing environment that represents everything they stand for artistically. 'We feel very lucky to be able to work together. We are very hands on, and even with interior projects we control the details by executing them ourselves. Next we would love to do a concept for a hotel.' My room is already booked.

See also pp. 268, 287
www.jamesplumb.co.uk

1

2

1 The 'Cluster' chandelier, a generous, cascading pendant, with lampshades of all shapes and sizes jostling for position.

2 'From This Day Forward' chair from the 'Concrete Stitches' series: broken and abandoned furniture rendered functional again by the casting of concrete in, on and around it.

3 Home sweet home: James Russell and Hannah Plumb live out their concept fully, applying their vision to their own home.

4 'Norman Webber' lamp created from an old paint kettle and lamp base, a piece from the 'Assemblages' series exhibited at the *From This Day Forward* exhibition, Milan, 2010.

5 An assemblage simply titled 'Book Sconce', also shown at the *From This Day Forward* exhibition.

6 There is a 'gipsy' or 'first settler' feel about James and Hannah's lovely kitchen, stacked with antique pieces.

7 Installation view of *From This Day Forward*, showing a campaign-style tent in which James and Hannah lived and slept during the exhibition.

8 A 'Cluster' chandelier hangs inside the tent, while on the outside a silkscreen luminaire has been mounted and two limited-edition dog lamps, 'Sampson' and 'Albie', pose on the rug.

9 The Hostem menswear shop in London, entirely fitted and interior-decorated by JAMESPLUMB.

10 & 11 Interior details in the Hostem menswear shop, London.

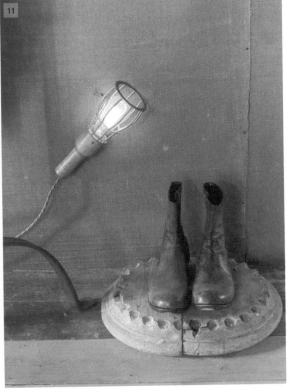

Janis Heezen

SWITZERLAND

Embroidery as textured drawing is an art form. This sort of needlework is not about embellishing a piece of clothing; rather, it is about conveying a pictorial message that has an emotional pull. It is a kind of painting, born out of labour-intensive sewing and stitching. Swiss embroidery, textile and paper artist Janis Heezen lives and works in Lucerne, but grew up in St Gallen, a town famous for its textile industry and embroidery tradition. Janis has been heavily influenced by her heritage and has long been fascinated by ancient handwork techniques and the possibility of interpreting them in new ways. Her sources of inspiration include embroidered textiles from the Swiss folk art tradition and from other traditional textile cultures all over the world. She is also inspired by the naïve art form known as *art brut*. She started out as a textile designer before deciding to study illustration at the College of Art and Design in Lucerne. Throughout her artistic career, however, textiles have never been far from her mind, and she has used her illustrative skills to bolster her embroidery ambitions. She started out by using cotton fabric as a base, either leaving it in a raw state or priming it with paint. The contrast between the lightness of the fabric and the imprint of her handicraft quickly became a source of enchantment for Janis. 'Due to the time-consuming process, embroidery turns out almost as an opportunity for me to meditate. As a result, my thoughts and dreams are firmly woven into my artworks. Each embroidery is a drawing delicately traced on the fabric, a reflection of my thoughts and inner pulse,' she muses. Technical and pigmentary references for Janis's work include the Edo-period woodcuts of Japanese artist Katsushika Hokusai and delicate, finely drawn Indian miniatures. The predominant themes that occupy Janis's artistic vision are beauty, the transience of life and death. 'Mostly it's an image that moves me in a strange way. It might be a doll's head, the feathers of a rare bird, or even the bark of a bare tree that stimulates my imagination and leads me to a precise idea. As the embroidery progresses, the figures start to develop a life of their own and begin telling their own story.' Janis's meticulous craft mimics that of an Old Master, with an embroidery needle in place of a paint brush.

See also p. 252
www.janisheezen.ch

1 Surrounded by her own drawings and inspirational items, Janis Heezen meticulously sets to work on her embroidery projects.

2 All projects start with a research phase, resulting in a collection of sketches, swatches and found images: these black scarabs were used for 'Home Sweet Home' (opposite).

3 Inspired by antique naval flags, 'Home Sweet Home' represents both homesickness and wanderlust, and was conceived for an exhibition called *Homeland*.

3

4 & 5 Fine sketches – the necessary stage before the embroidery begins – showcase Janis's exquisite drawing skills.

6 'Oiseaux' artwork, with embroidered details of budgerigars, whose feathers inspire a rich ornamental pattern.

7

8

7 'Kamakura Dancer' – a
female entertainer of the
twelfth-century Kamakura
period – was inspired by a
found picture, which Janis
transformed into something
new.

8 Can Janis turn anything into
gold? Her interior design
shares the extraordinary
flair of her embroidery:
this 'Golden Lace' artwork
perfectly complements the
domestic still life.

Jean Pelle
USA

Clever, beautiful objects that will improve our daily lives are not just a promise but a reality, made available by American designer Jean Pelle, who is based in Brooklyn, New York. Prior to founding her design studio, Jean worked at the offices of Tod Williams Billie Tsien Architects in New York, Eric Owen Moss Architects in Los Angeles and EHDD Architecture in San Francisco. She received her master's degree in architecture from Yale University, after a bachelor's in architecture from UC Berkeley. Fast forward to July 2008, when she changed tack to establish her own design studio. She started small, handcrafting a series of wooden candle-holders, though not your average holders, since 'Tod' and 'Dorit', for instance – your potential cool new best friends – came complete with a slick of 24-carat gold. First sold online, the candle-holders were quickly picked up by design boutiques across the US and became a key identifying piece of Jean's collection. Embracing her customers' enthusiasm, she accepted invitations to exhibit at several craft shows, including the *One of a Kind Show* in New York, where she received the Bloggers' Choice Award. Since then, Jean has continued to design and handcraft products that capture the imagination and showcase her approach to intelligent design.

Her interest in architecture and interiors has led her to create the 'Bubble Chandelier' series of lighting fixtures, as well as 'Button-Up', a folded cloth petal that opens to reveal a bulb, like a luminous stamen. With her 'Assemblage' series, Jean has also periodically released limited-edition items that are whimsical but useful, and include vanity cabinets, bedside trays and keepsake boxes. These are assembled from off-the-shelf parts that have been carefully re-imagined and re-composed by Jean to create new and unique, somehow personalized objects. The combination of intuitive craft production techniques and quality materials such as wood makes each of Jean's objects more than a useful functional product; they are valued companions to cherish.

See also pp. 266, 285, 297
www.jeanpelle.com

1 Long winter nights will become your favourite time of day thanks to the comforting glow of 'Tod' wooden candle-holders, stylishly slicked with 24-carat gold.

2 Organization is key: each component has its own box, and each box is shelved in the correct place.

3 Jean Pelle's studio is a multitasking artisan/designer showroom, in which brilliant creations – including 'Bubble' and 'Gold' chandeliers, and a 'Vanity Cabinet' – are displayed.

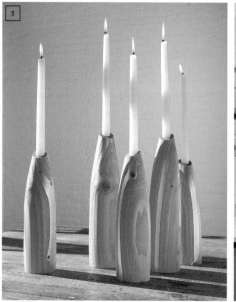

Jen Deschênes
UK

1 'Bunny Face' hand-embroidered
  vintage cotton cushion, with
  mother-of-pearl eye and
  handsome red fur pattern.

2 Introducing the gentleman/
  dandy/pirate: hand-
  screenprinted devoré cushion
  with hand-embroidery.

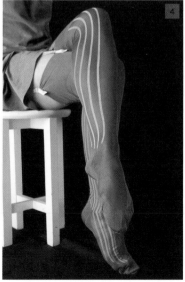

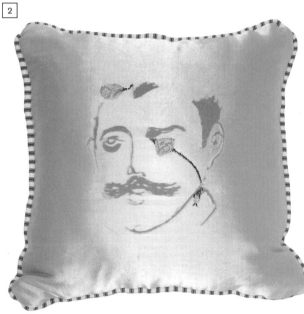

Hand woven genuine vintage stocking
By Jen Deschênes

Stockings

Stockings

3 Jen Deschênes
screenprinting in her
workshop, where her fabric
swatches, cushions and
children's dresses are all
within easy reach.

4 Stylish hand-screenprinted
vintage silk stockings.

5 Poo poo pi doo! Jen's
collection of elegant hand-
screenprinted vintage
(c. 1920–30) stockings, in
either real or artificial silk.

Expert hands are at work, precisely handling a
needle and firmly gripping the frame of a textile
canvas. One can follow every step of designer/
maker Jen Deschênes's creative process, thanks
to an 'immersive' video recording made possible
by HI-Arts Craft Development, whereby a camera
was devised for Jen to wear for a day while creating
her works in her studio in Lochaber in the Scottish
Highlands. Jen specializes in embroidery and
hand-screenprinting. She has always loved the
idea of 'making do' and of passing on history, so
her collections involve the re-working of vintage
fabrics and ephemera. Due to the materials' origins
and rarity, each piece she creates is unique. 'I
am interested in the intimacy of old fabric,' she
explains; 'to keep the character of the old cloth
but yet to infuse it with a new modernity and style.'
Jen was born and brought up on the island of
Whalsay in Shetland, and studied screenprinted
and embroidered textiles at Glasgow School of
Art and mixed-media textiles at the Royal College
of Art in London before moving to the Highlands.
'My work always has a narrative at its core, and
drawing is very important as a means of expressing
this,' she says. 'I love the naïvety and beauty of an

unfinished or rough drawing and like to translate
this into something well made, unique and beautiful.'
She is fascinated by antique embroidery transfers
and 'the idea of a print being an embroidery, or an
embroidery being a print'. This artistic approach
means that within each of Jen's creations – whether
her 'Bunny' cushion, whose simple embroidered
contours are finished with a big round vintage
button for the eye, or a pair of vintage silk stockings
hand-screenprinted with elegant stripes or bees,
or a poetic 'face brooch', whose characters are
adorable ladies from the 1920s – is embedded a
touch of nostalgia that ensures a tender appeal.
Jen 'recycles' treasures from the past, but she
rejuvenates them to the best of their potential.
They were always meant to be this beautiful, and
Jen's skilful embellishments just facilitate the
transformation.

See also pp. 268, 307
www.jendeschenes.co.uk

Jurianne Matter

NETHERLANDS

'As a little girl, I already knew that I wanted to become an "Inventor of Beautiful Things". I was constantly decorating, drawing, constructing machines, cutting paper and making music,' recalls designer and stylist Jurianne Matter. She attended one of the first Waldorf schools in the Netherlands, where her education was centred on respect for nature, art and spirituality. At home, anything was permitted so long as it was creative. Jurianne remembers covering lavatories in gold foil and painting furniture entirely white, with her parents' encouragement. In 1991, she graduated as one of the first students of the Interior Styling School at Artemis Academy in Amsterdam, a training that awakened her love of styling and her talent for inventing desirable objects. She held various creative jobs, including media stylist, concept and graphic designer, and stylist for IKEA Amsterdam, until tragedy struck and altered her path decisively. A much-loved friend and the friend's mother died in the tsunami of December 2004. The following year, as a way of commemorating the event,

Jurianne and her sons decided to draw, sign and fold paper boats and float them down the stream close to their holiday home. 'The sun was shining, and there they sailed away, our little wish boats,' Jurianne softly recalls. This was the beginning of a new passion: crafting little paper boats for special occasions such as anniversaries, weddings and birthdays. What began as the answer to a private emotional need became a successful business. Paper angels followed, then lanterns, then 'Blom', delicate ornamental paper flowers. But, as Jurianne points out, 'For me, a product is only beautiful if both nature and man have been considered in its development.' All of her products are made in the Netherlands and are eco-friendly. At their core they hold fine vibrant illustrative patterns, inspired by Jurianne's love of northern European hues and design, and by distinctive colour combinations that attract and energize her, as well as us.

See also pp. 1, 298
www.juriannematter.nl

1 A working still life: Jurianne Matter's ability to organize shapes and colours in harmony is an art.

2 Little 'Wish Boats' help to mark special occasions: give your boat a name, write a personal wish or message on it, and let it sail away.

1

Jurianne Matter

3 Jurianne's florist kit: the clippers and thin wire used to create 'Blom' flower stems.

4 Tool of the trade: a special magnifying glass, here being used to check the alignment of different colour layers.

5 Industrial dies for 'Blom' flowers: after the floral paper has been printed, it is sent to the die-cutter.

6 Springtime in Paperland: each delicately patterned and cheerfully hued flower is unique.

7 Note down a wish or a greeting on the heart of an 'Angel' and let the magic happen.

8 A 'Lantern' with a message can become an invitation, a get-well card, a birthday greeting or a steadfast companion in dark times.

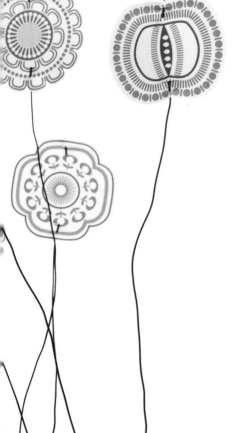

Krasznai

SPAIN

1 Quirkiness at its most functional: the 'Tin' baking container is a baby whose giggling may erupt as soon as you plunge that spoon into the cake.

2 How can one resist? 'Hold me!', 'Pick an olive!' this adorable porcelain bowl seems to beg.

3 Krasznai's porcelain bowls, cups, vases and little sculptures seem quite 'harmless' when waiting in line to be fitted with their baby arms.

4 Finished vessels and decorative objects comprise a brave little army of porcelain huggers.

While visiting Budapest a few years ago, Roger Coll bought a street sign saying 'Krasznai Utca', or Krasznai Street. Not knowing exactly what it meant, he kept it next to his old kiln. He subsequently found out that 'Krasznai' literally means 'from Kraszna', a town in Hungary. Some time later, for an exhibition in Barcelona, he decided to hang his artworks outside, on an imaginary Krasznai street. He named his collection after the town, and so Krasznai ceramics was born. 'I realize it's not an easy name to remember. I've seen it written as Kraznai, Karszai, Kransai ... and I always find it funny!' laughs Roger. Before setting up his studio, he spent several years studying and working in sculpture, ceramics and technical architecture, including a stint in Helsinki on a sculpture scholarship. On his return, he established his studio in Badalona, near Barcelona, and that is where he handmakes all his creations from start to finish. He relies heavily on a pool of creative friends – including Nika Hellström, Marc Sanchez, Marta Monsarro and Artur Muñoz – to share ideas. However, his trademark 'Arms&Crafts' series came about almost by accident. During a summer vacation in Portugal, Roger found a toy arm poking out of the sand on the beach. He kept it in his studio, between vases and other objects, always within reach. At some point, he got the idea that he could paste arms onto a vase, thereby giving the vessel a humorous yet emotive quality. 'I wouldn't dare to say there is a deeper meaning behind "Arms&Crafts",' he now says. 'What it does is put a smile on people's faces.' There may not be a deeper meaning, but the series definitely has a higher purpose, in that it draws people into the world of ceramics by showing that anything is possible. 'It is a captivating form of artisanship,' Roger enthuses, 'with a lot of potential to unleash creativity. I strive to make people appreciate handmade objects that take time to produce, now that everything is digital.' Gazing at his functional vessels with their little outstretched arms, we hear the words 'Come closer', 'Hug me' or 'Hold me'. How can we resist these fabulous creations?

See also p. 303
www.krasznai.co.uk

Kristin Lora

USA

1 The 'Dog Training Class' music box, hand-fabricated with oxidized sterling silver, music-box parts, train-set figures and found objects.

2 'Felt Ball' cufflinks, or how to fit a circle in a square: oxidized sterling silver with handmade wool felt balls.

3 The multicoloured 'Felt Ball' bracelet is the perfect combination of sturdy preciousness and light crafty fun, in sterling silver with handmade wool felt balls.

4 Kristin Lora's work-table is an arresting sight. Plastic animals are beheaded and dismembered for a higher purpose – whimsical, get-you-noticed pieces of jewelry.

4

Add a lighthearted touch to the day by wearing a bracelet on which tiny figures are enjoying a train ride, or a necklace on which miniature swimmers are keeping fit … unless you opt for a colourful yet sleek silver brooch with round felt balls. Or how about listening to soothing tunes spilling out of a music box on which a lively Lilliputian scene runs unbridled? Bold lines and an upfront whimsy prevail in the jewelry and small-scale sculptures of American artist Kristin Lora. Her imagery includes scaled-down replicas of objects with which she is familiar (such as vehicles) and objects she invents in her mind (aliens and other creatures). Before learning metalwork, Kristin gained a degree in zoology. Tiny toys and sculptural jewelry are now her favourite avenues for creativity. 'I love the intimate scale that this work provides, both as the maker and as a viewer. I love watching the reaction of discovery when others notice the tiny and unexpected details within my pieces.' Kristin is very sensitive to shapes, textures and finishes, and views everything she sees in terms of reference to her work. 'I collect objects, new and used, and keep them in my studio for inspiration, and they often sit on my shelves until an idea just comes to me one day,' she says. Motion is a key element and Kristin

enjoys creating the mechanisms that allow it. Humour is also a paramount concept, in both her work and her life – a very direct humour that is slightly bemused. Kristin primarily works in precious metals, and she mainly combines them with found objects. She utilizes a variety of traditional metal- and silversmithing techniques, including soldering, riveting, raising, dapping, forging and stone-setting. All of her jewelry, functional objects and sculptures are fabricated by hand. 'I prefer to do one-of-a-kind pieces. If I choose to duplicate a previous design, there are always subtle differences in the subsequent work,' she states. Kristin's artistic journey, begun when she was a small child, has continued throughout the years, as she has experimented with beading, ceramics, sewing, textiles, glass, painting, sculpture, music and more. 'What I like best is creating something that has never existed before,' she says. Her work is now rightfully celebrated, as attested by the multiple exhibitions and publications in which her joyful creations have made an appearance.

See also pp. 281, 283
www.kristinlora.com

Kristin Lora

5 Kristin in her busy workshop, highly representative of her ebullient mind and animated craft style.

6 Nothing is wasted and everything is saved for Kristin's uncanny talent for telling stories with just a few miniature parts.

7 Crack a smile from your audience with the 'Shadowbox' pendant featuring train-set swimmers, oxidized sterling silver, Lucite balls and watch crystals.

8 This tiny tourist couple will certainly do a lot of sightseeing attached to your finger: the 'Car' ring is hand-fabricated with antiqued sterling silver, train-set figures and cubic zirconia.

9 Commuting transformed into escapism: the 'Commuter Train' bracelet of oxidized sterling silver and resin, with train-set figures.

10 The attention to detail is riveting in this 'Air Stream Trailer' toy, hand-fabricated with sterling silver, train-set figures, cubic zirconia and garnets.

7

8

9

10

Kristina Klarin

ITALY

'Unique' and 'handmade' are two concepts that are often mentioned together, but they have seldom been so in tune as in the work of Kristina Klarin. Born in Belgrade, Kristina studied textile design before moving to Italy's fashion capital, Milan, where she graduated in fashion design from the Marangoni Institute. After working with several renowned fashion companies and learning about different aspects of the industry, 'including the dark side', Kristina realized that she was meant to express her creativity differently. Her fascination for the pre-Industrial Revolution period, when artisans were both designers and manufacturers, led her to recognize that, for her, the most beautiful part of the creative process was the making of prototypes from initial drawings. During the course of her new journey into artisanship, Kristina came across a huge online community of like-minded people, which prompted her to launch her own blog, 'Kris's colour stripes', as a way of keeping an intimate diary of creative observations, cherished inspirations and happy experiments with colour. She was, and still is, driven by the idea of inspiring others 'to use colours playfully and not just as a rigid scheme'. Consequently, and in a logical 'put in practice what I preach' way, her delightful jewelry line is primarily focused on well-balanced, sophisticated colours. Her necklaces are crafted using natural materials such as wood, cotton and eco paint, and are entirely handmade from start to finish. Some are strikingly elegant and refined; others more flamboyant and fun. One can see the influence of interior designers such as Charles and Ray Eames and George Nelson, and painters such as Sonia Delaunay, rather than that of fashion designers. With her exquisite craft, Kristina has succeeded in creating a line that transcends trends, dispels boredom, and brings conscientious thinking and production back into fashion. Bravo!

See also p. 274
http://kristinaklarin.blogspot.com

1 Kristina Klarin hand-stamping cotton for a necklace with brightly coloured dots. The cotton is ruched in between wooden beads to give a collar aspect to the finished object.

2 So tempting, they seem almost edible: wooden beads dipped into paint, then left to set and dry, like candy skewers.

3 Birth of a neckpiece: a story board, sketches, swatches and colour references to find the perfect balance between colour and shape.

4 Like a breath of extra fresh air, the pale green, eggshell blue, leaf green and aubergine combination of this necklace attests to Kristina's fine colour sense.

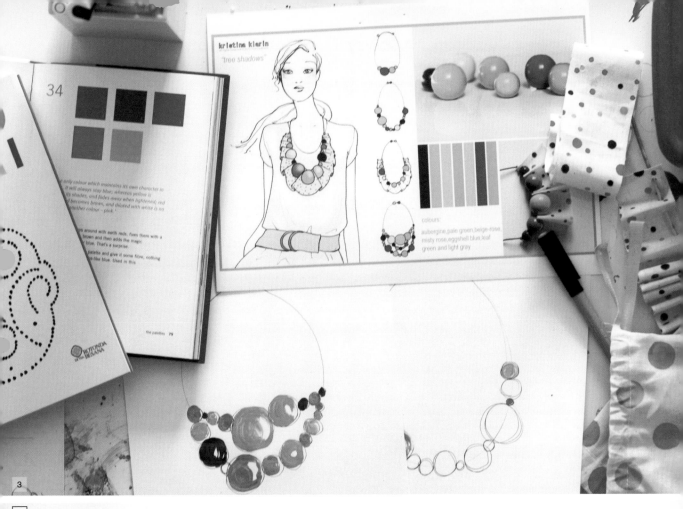

34

...only colour which maintains its own character in... It will always stay blue; whereas yellow is ...its shades, and fades away when lightened; red ...becomes brown, and diluted with white is no ...another colour – pink."

...ers around with earth reds, fixes them with a ...brown and then adds the magic: ...r blue. That's a surprise.

...palette and give it some fibre, nothing ...e-like blue. Used in this

the palette **79**

kristina klarin
"tree shadows"

colours:
aubergine,pale green,beige-rose,
misty rose,eggshell blue,leaf
green and light gray

3

4

Lars Rank

DENMARK

Danish ceramicist Lars Rank does practically everything himself. His passion for ceramics began in his early twenties, when he attended a pottery course. This was the turning point that led him to enrol at the Jutland Art Academy in Aarhus. There he worked on projects that were a blend of art and design, but always involved ceramics. During this period, he created his 'Containers' series out of ceramic casts of disposable food packaging. Henceforth, he was to devote himself to creating functional products. A four-month residency at the Shigaraki Ceramic Cultural Park gave him a rare opportunity to explore Japanese craft traditions, and these also inspired his way of approaching design. 'Interaction, passion and diversity are key words for my work,' says Lars. All of his products are cast in porcelain and processed by hand with precision and dedication. His designs often consist of a clean form, but with a decoration as a surprise. Take the 'Sta'vase', a candle-holder or a vase, which has its upper third worked on with several layers of crystalline glaze. When fired, the glaze runs down in drips, forming pools around the holder. 'The design process is an interaction between the ceramic material and the idea,' Lars notes. 'It's not so much about controlling the ceramic material, but more about giving it a context in which to unfold. Consequently, I don't get two objects that are the same.' Lars is able to offer what large, mass-producing companies cannot, and that is design with variety. For example, all the dots in his 'Dots' tableware collection are made with coloured slip in the slipcasting process and, as a result, every dot is unique and the colour combinations are endless. Just as striking is Lars's 'Tilted Lighthouse' tealight-holder, which looks like a miniature model of a very modern building. Cast in translucent Parian porcelain, each holder consists of three cylindrical rings that are stacked and staggered horizontally on top of one other. Meanwhile, Lars's 'Weeds' series of two tealight-holders and two pendant lights uses dried plants that are cast into the Parian porcelain. When lit up, the light source glows in warm orange and the plants appear as beautiful, luminous silhouettes. Lars's enchanting objects have an incredibly soothing effect: ceramics as source of wellbeing.

See also pp. 262, 287, 305
www.rank.dk

1

1 The 'Containers' series: ceramic casts of everyday disposable food packages.

2 Calm and order reign inside the kiln.

3 Lars Rank casts a bowl in porcelain by pouring liquid clay into round moulds; once each mould is filled to the top, it sits for a certain amount of time depending on the thickness desired for the edges.

4 Pieces from the 'Dots' series, ready to be glazed.

Lars Rank

5 'Dots' playfully reinterprets tableware by offering fourteen hand-decorated multifunctional parts, in six different colourways, with dots in various sizes and colours. Mix and match your crockery in a multitude of shape and colour combinations.

6 'Classic' hearts, pine trees and stars handmade in porcelain to celebrate Christmas with Nordic simplicity and modern style.

7 Clever design with a name that says it all: 'Sta'vase' is a contraction of the Danish words for 'candle-holder' and 'vase'.

5

Laura Strasser

GERMANY

1 'Service Blanche with Rice Decoration' takes up the traditional Asian rice-grain porcelain pattern. The holes left by grains of rice fired in the kiln are filled with glaze that remains translucent when the ceramics are fired again.

2 The '14%' light makes use of the fact that porcelain shrinks during glaze firing. Each lampshade is a cast of the previous, larger shade.

3 'With Love From China: originals are becoming rarer, safeguard your copy!': Laura Strasser contacted Chinese manufacturers to reproduce copies of her own portrait.

4 Laura removing a '14%' light from its mould.

White porcelain tableware joins not-so-traditional portrait busts and sleek pendant lights to form a collection of elegant, functional sculptures. Laura Strasser, the creator of this audacious ceramic celebration, lives and works in Weimar, Germany. After a period as a stage designer in Frankfurt, she moved to Weimar to study product design at the Bauhaus University, before being awarded a scholarship to the Pratt Institute in New York. This was where she first came across porcelain work, under the invaluable coaching of ceramic artist Irvin Tepper. The encounter propelled Laura's artistic drive in a new direction. From then on, she would be fascinated by white porcelain and would almost exclusively develop themes around this noble material. Collaborative work has been a strong component of her career. Since 2006, she has worked with KAHLA Thüringen Porzellan, under the mentorship of the porcelain designer Barbara Schmidt. She has also co-founded a small design label, Frenchnicker, with fellow designer Milia Seyppel. Periodically Laura holds workshops at the Bauhaus University, and, in 2009, she co-founded 'My Bauhaus Is Better Than Yours', an exhibition platform to present and promote the works of graduates and young designers from the university. In addition, Laura is involved in organizing several socially interactive projects, including 'Omarillio', an art festival in Weimar, and the gallery marke.6 at the Neuen Museum Weimar. Nonetheless she manages to make time for her own projects. Her preferred craft technique is slipcasting, and she works by hand in plaster, her forms freely modelled or thrown on a plaster wheel. Her work engages with the characteristics and potentialities of porcelain, as well as the social and historical meaning of the material. By opting for creations with contemporary and humorous names, such as '14%', 'Trauma', 'Quadrature' and 'With Love From China', Laura seeks to reach new aesthetic standards while simultaneously challenging people's understanding and perceptions. Her in-depth research also provides a rich conceptual substance to her craft. Through her work, she aims to achieve nothing less than the extraction, re-interpretation and translation of a centuries-long tradition into a product for our own time. Long-lasting, handmade, desirable and meaningful craft: a winner.

See also pp. 261, 285, 287, 302
www.laura-strasser.de

Lena Levchenko

UKRAINE

1

The sculptor Camille Claudel once said something to the effect of: 'People learn about the world not by taking from it, but by enriching it.' This is Lena Levchenko's main creative motto. Her artistic journey began when she enrolled at an art college in the Ukraine. There she applied herself to learning indigenous folk embroidery, a tradition with both spiritual and material meaning for Ukrainians. Knowing about her native embroidery history helped Lena explore the thoughts and emotions conveyed by generations of Ukrainian artists. During her studies she took part in various exhibitions and competitions, and she was always active on the local art scene, helping designers to implement creative ideas and leading workshops for children. Avant-garde artists such as Alexandra Exter, Liubov Popova, Olga Rozanova and Nadezhda Udaltsova inspired her first womenswear collection. 'I tried to express myself through embroidery work for dresses and jackets, jewelry and pretty accessories, greeting cards and crocheted toys,' says Lena. Once she realized that people liked her work, she decided to set up as a designer with 'Nabnable', her contemporary brand of handmade interior-decoration items and fashion accessories.

The way Lena designs depends on what her customers order. She tries to tailor her creations to people's needs. Whether a cushion, a baby gift or a traditional embroidered piece of linen, her works demonstrate extraordinary technical skill in the complex construction of beautiful patterns by hand. They even channel the state of mind she is in while crafting each piece. 'I look at the bright side of things and incarnate it in my works. I derive my motivation and energy for self-perfection from art, music, films and poetry. Working on a new project, I fully give myself up to inspiration. Even the smallest trinket that I create carries a part of my soul,' she confides. Lena understands that her work may not have a huge impact on people's lives, but she believes that it is a small contribution towards improving aesthetic taste, and, to a certain extent, enriching the world around her. By revitalizing a traditional craft, she has succeeded in preserving the past folklore of her country while placing it firmly in modern times. Artisanship as patriotic endeavour: what country could not benefit from this positive, alternative kind of exposure?

See also pp. 308, 310
www.nabnable.com

1 The first stage of any embroidery is the sketch, defining the parameters and placement for the best possible result.

2 Get in line for the hand-crocheted 'Chicken' dance.

3 These quirky, handmade bird ornaments have a distinctive crafty aspect, yet also a modern edge.

4 A placid cat, handmade in cotton, serves as a cosy pillow or cuddly toy.

5 Traditional Ukrainian embroideries in cotton and viscose are made contemporary in Lena Levchenko's collection of colourful, graphic, highly decorative cushions.

2

Lyndie Dourthe

FRANCE

Welcome to a new kind of Wonderland. It is French, and it is in Paris. In this unique and captivating world, fabrics and paper combine to form a poetic, mysterious and sometimes bizarre array of naturalistic wonders. Lyndie Dourthe – she could have been a nineteenth-century entomologist, biologist or anthropologist – compulsively collects lovely treasures in labelled jars, the sources for creating her meticulous and delicate pieces. We have a definite sense of being in the presence of someone who is curating an intimate, contemporary cabinet of curiosities; a unique congregation and combination of flora, fauna and anatomy, all topped with a zest of voodoo. As Lyndie readily admits, she is 'inspired, fascinated by and obsessed with natural history sciences. I can't help delving into botany, anatomy, insects and animals, and more recently vanities and ex-votos.' Necklaces, brooches, boxes, clocks and mobiles, all her precious creations have a charm and a magical quality. They are genuine talismans that cast the spell of childhood visions. Lyndie's vivid imagination races all year long, and she often ends up reinterpreting elements of nature through intriguing yet beautiful hybrids. Along with the enchanting quality that permeates her work, one can also find grace and sensuality. Lyndie is a colour expert, and she embraces nature's most subtle palettes for her projects. Each piece is the outcome of a long and precise manual construction process. She cuts, dyes, assembles, plies, beads and sews each one-off wonder herself, in a cavernous, Ali Baba-esque workshop. Some projects take months to complete, such as the huge glass domes that private collectors commission her to decorate according to their specific themes, or the window displays that in-the-know shops ask her to design and build from scratch. Lyndie's talent is enviable, and her work is deliciously addictive. If that doesn't define spellbinding, what does?

See also pp. 277, 314
http://lyndiedourthe.monsite-orange.fr

1 A collection of glass cases and cloches adorns the window of a Parisian shop, each containing a unique handmade wonder.

2 The walls of Lyndie Dourthe's workshop are covered with inspirational notes and images, as well as intriguing paraphernalia.

3 A textile couple from the 'Les Ecorchés, Anatomie' collection, who have been stripped down to the ultimate nudity: the man remains modest and looks the other way.

4 This gentle skeleton of bead-embroidered printed cotton seems to be meditating on the little butterflies that fly freely around its glass home.

5 Precise craftwork gives Lyndie's pieces a little soul: each detachable organ, printed on cotton, is hand-sewn and sometimes adorned with beads.

2

3

4

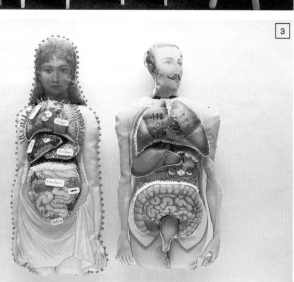

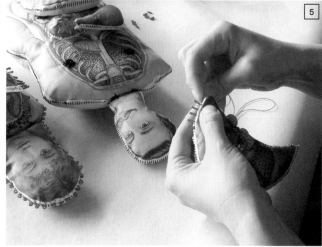

5

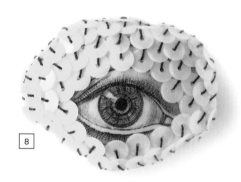

6 Printed cotton 'Champignon' brooches are gathered under a glass dome to create an appetizing but dangerous undergrowth scene.

7 The passing of time is beautifully captured in this 'Vanitas' pear piece, a print on cotton with musty green beads and a little pinned fly.

8 'Look me in the eye!' says this 'Ex Voto' graphic brooch, adorned with bright yellow sequins and jet black thread.

9 Wear your heart on your sleeve with this beaded and sequinned brooch from the 'Anatomie Graphique' collection.

10 Brooch characters from the 'Les Ecorchés, Anatomie' collection, in boxes lined with fine cotton gauze.

11 Read your fortune on 'Lignes de la Main' brooches, printed on cotton with palm-lines indicated by little name tags.

12 Forget me not: a printed skull brooch adorned with pansies (the brooch is delivered in a cotton organdie origami pouch).

9

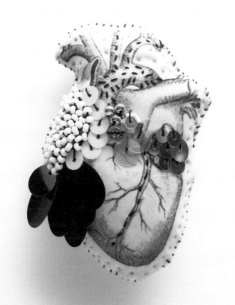

10

11

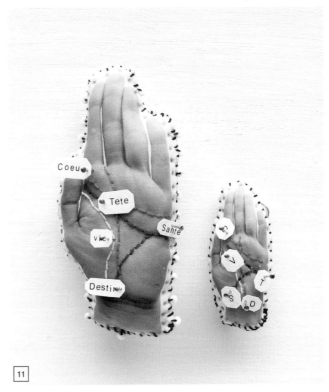

Coeu

Tete

Vice

Sante

Desti

12

Manon Gignoux

FRANCE

The origins of Manon Gignoux's evocative work can be traced back to her last year of study at the Duperré School of Applied Arts in Paris. There she carried out two insightful photographic studies: one an investigation of the inner, imaginary realm of a family home, and the other a study of the 'traces of wear and tear' on the clothes worn by workers in the early twentieth century. Manon explored the signs of alteration, the imprint of repeated movements, the dynamics of construction and the way in which a worn object fits the body. These early conceptual projects shaped her vision and her artistic approach to textiles. 'I create one-off fabric sculptures, dressed objects, clothes and accessories, each piece being unique,' she says. 'My creations illustrate the meeting of clothes, body and decor, each becoming an intimate vessel for the passing of time.' She has created costumes for contemporary dance, theatre and circus companies, notably for the Théâtre de l'Odéon in Paris and for James Thiérrée at the Théâtre de la Ville and Julie Brochen at the Théâtre National de Strasbourg. She also lectures at several art schools in France. For her work, Manon sources raw materials with three concepts in mind: recovery, reappropriation and aesthetic discrepancy. The clothes and objects she finds are previously owned and retain the memory of their original usage. She combines them with contemporary fabrics that are reworked with dyes and pleats. Manon's poetic transformation confers upon her raw materials a new function and identity. Her clothes pass on the experience of living, flattering and also somehow deforming the body. Her textile objects, such as her fabric dolls, have a symbolic value, with their own particular personalities. 'I play on the relationship between clothes and objects. I also set up installations in which I associate my work with found objects, reinvented and/or photographed,' she explains. Her creations have been exhibited both nationally and internationally – notably in Marithé + François Girbaud's shop windows – and are in the collection of the Galliera Museum of Fashion in Paris. Manon's intentions may be solely artistic, but it just so happens that some clients – collectors and textile enthusiasts – not only admire her sculpted clothes and accessories, but also wear them. Once elevated to an art form by Manon, her pieces instil an irresistible desire in some followers, and that says a lot about their creator's bewitching ability to infuse timeless beauty in her reborn pieces.

See also p. 320
www.manon-gignoux.com

1 Manon Gignoux's workshop is a serene setting for her suspended textile sculptures and her collection of ephemera, serving as both inspirational and work material.

2 A poetic textile composition made with tatters of fabric interweaved with items of clothing.

3 Unique 'Objets emmaillotés', or 'Dressed objects', encompass the notion of the passing of time.

4 Found treasures of textile and paper, yet to be transformed and recycled into symbolic creations.

5 A spectacularly intricate 'Entrelacement' jacket, both textile sculpture and one-of-a-kind garment.

6 These textile sculptures on hangers seem to have a life of their own.

7 Mysterious, eerie silhouettes make up the textile sculpture 'n'Être', whose title reads in French both as 'to be born' (*naître*) or 'not to be' (*n'être*).

8 A rag doll sculpture dressed with a lush flouncing scarf.

9 Years of careful collecting and working with rare textiles are neatly represented in Manon's workshop racks and shelves.

Maria Jauhiainen

FINLAND

1 Tools, bits and pieces of wire and inspirational mementos are all jumbled together to create a cheerful and feminine tableau.

2 'Hearts Screen', a metal work-in-progress, floats in the air, seeming to confirm its extraordinary lightness.

3 This close-up of 'Hearts Screen' shows how the clever positioning of each heart plays with light, both reflecting the gleam of metal and casting delicate shadows.

4 Backbones of the screen: Maria Jauhiainen reveals the way in which her hundreds of diaphanous shapes are welded together to form a robust, wide, lace-like structure.

Nature is known for its precision and perfection, and natural forms, shades and associations have an inherent beauty that is a constant source of inspiration to many. However, only a few have truly been able to capture its essence, and even fewer are gifted enough to be able to replicate its architectural and structural splendour. Maria Jauhiainen is one. This Finnish metalsmith designs and creates showstopping pieces of jewelry and decorative objects, which mimic as well as sublimate natural elements. Maria has a highly distinctive style, which she has developed through her in-depth knowledge of metalworking processes and techniques, and through her obsessive study of delicate natural structures (she has a particular predilection for ginkgo leaves). After obtaining a degree in silversmithing from the Lahti Design Institute, Maria moved to London to study for her master's degree at the Royal College of Art. Since graduating, she has worked and exhibited as an independent designer, and her creations have been acquired by some of the world's most eminent museums, including the Museum of Modern Art

in New York, the Victoria and Albert Museum in London and the Musée des Arts Décoratifs in Paris. Maria has also held two prestigious artist-in-residency positions: one at the Cité des Arts in Paris, and the other at the Finnish Cultural Institute in New York. 'Curiosity is the driving force behind my work,' she explains. 'I want to understand how things work and why certain choices are made. Through the study of nature, universal patterns emerge, from the veins of a leaf to patterns of thought.' Her gossamer-light metal pieces are functional items that appear to be too delicate to use but are actually surprisingly strong and flexible to the touch. In her work, through astute experimentation, she has mastered the ability to create lace-like structures that not only retain their strength but also interact beautifully with light. 'I am interested in the characteristics of metal. Often heft and weight are associated with the value of a metal object. I like to see how light a structure can become without breaking, and in that way show the sensitivity and strength of metal.' This is precisely Maria's great achievement and paradox. In exploiting the robustness and malleability of metal, she has distilled a natural diaphanous beauty: the essence, but not the reality, of fragility.

See also p. 290
maria.jauhiainen@talk21.com

Marie Christophe

FRANCE

Sculpting in the air with a humble cable and creating elegant structures and characters with a powerful poetic spirit is Marie Christophe's enchanting skill. Some of her creations remain artistic, to be beheld and admired; others take a functional route, when adorned with bulbs and turned into chandeliers. Based in Paris, Marie works in a bright studio, where wires, beads and stones wait to be appointed to their higher destiny. She attributes her interest in design and art to her father, an architect with a passion for Japanese gardens and African art. Marie confides that 'a good design is for me to get the right balance between style and substance, so that the object organically finds its inherent function, be it aesthetic or utilitarian. However, I consider myself a creative artisan rather than a designer.' Marie initially chose iron wire purely for practical reasons, but, loving its great pliability, she has never sought to replace it. She does, however, manipulate complementary materials, such as crystal and ceramics, which enable her to introduce colour. 'Travels, temporary exhibitions and fabrics all inspire me. I keep little notebooks in which I draw, collect and collage ideas. It is absolutely vital to remain open and curious about what is around us,' says Marie. Her creative process always starts with a drawing

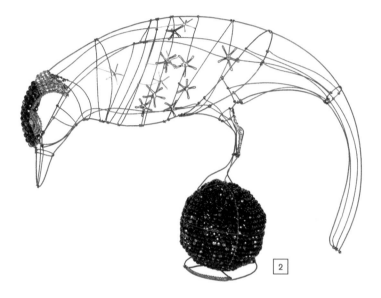

phase. She skips the model-making stage, preferring to dive straight into the making phase. 'The crucial moment is when a sculpture finally morphs into an animal or an object; when it gets its recognizable and ultimate identity,' she enthuses. Marie's work enhances any space. Luxury houses, including Louis Vuitton, Hermès and Cartier, have identified her unique ability and commissioned her to fit out their windows and shop interiors. She also collaborates with architects and interior designers to decorate hotels (for example, La Belle Juliette in Paris), spas and houses for private clients. Marie's ultimate dream is 'to be given carte blanche for the embellishment of a huge empty space in Paris, Tokyo or New York City'. One might think that her own residence would cascade with her creations, giant creatures and gorgeous candelabras everywhere. In fact, she has just a few simple pieces, little envoys from her workshop. She keeps the spectacular numbers for us.

See also pp. 253, 288
www.mariechristophe.com

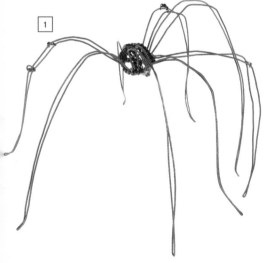

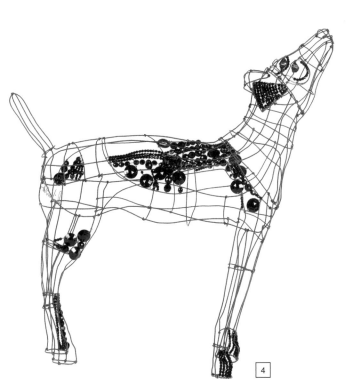

1 Wire is an excellent material for embodying the light spindliness of a super-long-legged spider.

2 A bird sculpture, regally perched on a beaded ball, seems to have found a tight equilibrium.

3 It looks like Christmas every day in Marie Christophe's workshop, as this detail of a shelf confirms, with its delicate wire creations and stylish ephemera.

4 Black beading is artistically positioned to create a patchy fur-like coat on this dog sculpture.

149

5 Watch your head, you
  might bump into one of
  these exquisite chandelier
  creations – part finished
  orders, part works-in-
  progress.

6 Marie uses several different-
  sized pliers to assemble her
  wire pieces, including this
  bee, whose head and body
  are entirely beaded.

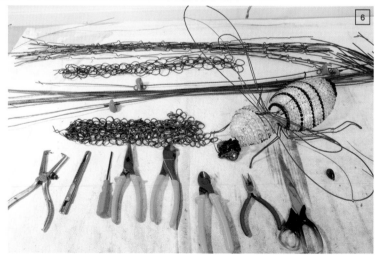

7

7 One can clearly see why
Marie works with a smile
on her face: her workshop
abounds with lighthearted
sculptures and pleasing
lamps.

8 This bejewelled beetle
sculpture would cure
anyone of insect phobia.

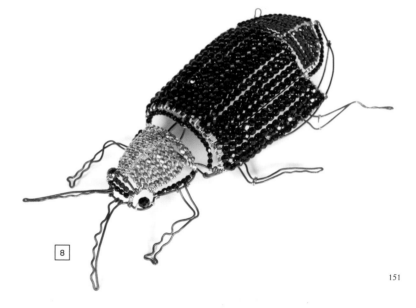

8

Mel Robson

AUSTRALIA

Mel Robson is a ceramicist, an artist and a storyteller. Most of her work has a strong narrative component, and she is fascinated by the ways in which we record and remember our stories. 'I often explore this in the context of my own family history,' she confides. 'I like working with objects that already exist and building upon their existing history by adding a little more of my own story to them.' Mel is particularly interested in the associations that can become attached to utilitarian objects, and the ways in which these objects can then evoke memories or create connections between the past and the present. From her Alice Springs base, she creates delicate pieces out of porcelain, her material of choice. 'It's just so clean and white, light and versatile, evocative, classic and contemporary all at the same time; qualities I strive to achieve in my work,' she says. Her collection includes both functional and decorative items for the home, limited-edition pieces and one-off exhibition works. 'What drew me to ceramics was the idea of utility, the idea of making useful things. That's still important to me, although my practice has developed from a mostly functional focus to a broader sculptural practice. The functional domestic object, however, still remains at the heart of my work and is the starting point for most of what I make,' she states. Her work has been featured in numerous publications, and she has been selected twice for the prestigious World Ceramics Biennale in South Korea and the International Ceramics Festival in Mino, Japan. Recently she was commissioned by the State government to make a work in commemoration of one hundred years of women's suffrage in Queensland, an opportunity to access some extraordinary archival material and to spend a few months researching the history of the women's movement in her home state. Her porcelain works are slipcast and decorated with original designs and hand-drawings, as well as imagery sourced from old photographs, maps, recipes, personal letters, vintage fabrics and wallpapers. This imagery is transformed into ceramic decals, which are applied by hand and permanently fired onto the fine porcelain. Mel's work revolves around nostalgia. Her evocative but contemporary pieces, projecting a deceptive fragility and a quiet dark humour, skilfully weave together stories that play with our ideas of time.

See also pp. 257, 301
http://feffakookan.blogspot.com

1 Mel Robson's splattered
   throwing bats and the
   potter's wheel where she
   throws vessels and forms for
   making moulds.

2 The tools of the trade include
   glaze tongs, paintbrushes
   for glazing pots and turning
   tools for thrown vessels.

3 Function meets sculpture:
   'By Hand', press-moulded
   porcelain and stoneware with
   decals.

4 Mel's experimental wall, with
   clay thumbprints, pictures
   of her ceramics and three
   porcelain tiles inspired by
   images on the wall.

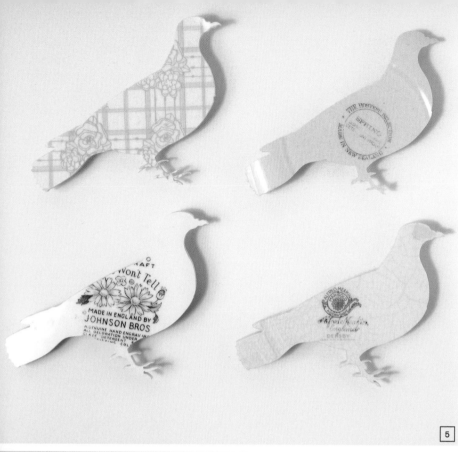

5 Extracting new avian life out of discarded old wares: 'You are My Sunshine', made with found ceramic plates.

6 A utilitarian ceramic plate has been waterjet-cut, transforming it into 'Shot Gun', a clever and dramatic conceptual artwork.

7 There is a dose of dark humour in Mel's poetic reinterpretations: 'Keep Calm and Carry On (Gun)', in slipcast porcelain.

8 Ceramics can also be used to convey a political message: 'Fight and Flight', slipcast porcelain with decals.

6 7

8

9 Decals beautifully enhance the translucent quality of Mel's slipcast porcelain 'Recipe Bowl'.

10 The 'Patchwork' series in slipcast porcelain with decals conveys Mel's predilection for a nostalgic approach.

9

10

Melanie Bilenker

USA

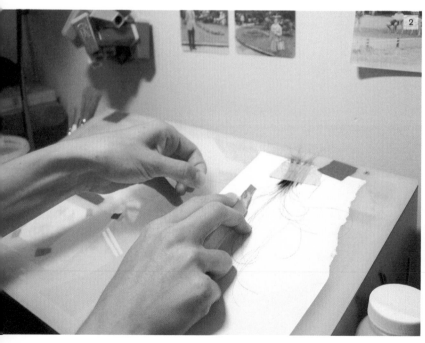

The fear of forgetting is a powerful force behind the work of Melanie Bilenker, an American jewelry maker and artist, who captures the mundane, the domestic, the ordinary in intricate pieces of jewelry: miniature portraits as snapshots frozen in time. Melanie is most captivated by jewelry that has been passed down through families, the pieces that tell of personal relationships, the pieces imbued with memories. This interest drew her to Victorian jewelry and the use of hair as a physical stand-in for a person, most commonly a lover or deceased family member. However, Melanie does not use hair to memorialize love or death but, rather, the small, banal moments we all experience. As she says: 'I commemorate the commonplace. It is the quiet moments that make up the whole of our lives. And I enjoy the universality of such common images.' The Victorians kept lockets of hair and miniatures painted with ground hair and pigment to secure the memory of a lost love. In much the same way, Melanie secures her memories through photographic imagery rendered in strands of her own hair. 'I am very interested in commemoration,' she notes. 'For this reason, I have always loved sentimental jewelry, love tokens, charm bracelets, cheap plastic souvenirs.' She collects amateur vintage snapshots and also looks to contemporary photography for inspiration. She particularly appreciates images that illustrate traces or evidence of people. Of the German artist Hans Peter-Feldmann, she enthuses, 'He has one series called "All the Clothes of a Woman", in which he shot a portrait of each article of one woman's wardrobe, resulting in her portrait in absentia. In these photographs there is a sense of voyeurism, which also draws me to look at found snapshots. They are so very intimate. Similarly, hair is an intimate material, as it speaks to privacy and domesticity.' Melanie spends a lot of time thinking about what is left behind, whether this be an image or a physical trace. As such, she is intrigued by what people choose to record. Most people take photographs of significant events, but what really interests her are the images of mundane everyday things. Her favourite quote is from the French philosopher Henri Lefebvre, who once stated that he was not interested in the high points of life, that only five minutes of every day are interesting, and that he wanted to show the rest; 'normal life'.

See also p. 278
www.melaniebilenker.com

1 Do not be fooled: amazingly, the fine lines Melanie Bilenker has used to depict herself playing solitaire are not made with pencil but with human hair.

2 The making of each brooch is almost comparable to a surgical procedure, starting with the precise separation and cutting to length of individual strands of hair.

3 A glimpse of Melanie's collection of antique, or 'memory', tokens, which resonate with traces or evidence of people.

4 'Tucking', a comely example of the way in which Melanie commemorates the mundane, freezing the moment as in a snapshot.

5 The pleasure of voyeurism: an intimate moment captured in 'Hemming Pants'.

4

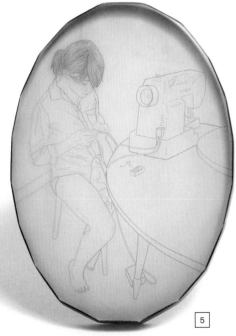

5

Nathalie Choux
FRANCE

Some ceramicists claim that they fell in love with earthenware because of its endless challenges and possibilities; others recall a revelation, like a bolt of lightning striking them with a passion. French artist Nathalie Choux chose ceramics for a different and more practical reason: necessity. 'I had to have my own china,' she cries, 'so unique that nothing similar could be found in any shop; so appealing that my guests would be consumed with envy!' Nathalie is an illustrator by profession, and she has effortlessly transferred her visions onto her porcelain creations. She is convinced that *l'art de la table* – the art of tableware – is like art direction. It must be about creating a cohesive scene and having the different elements – plates, bowls, cups – be the actors in a story. 'Coming from an illustrative background, I am pretty sure it is a force of habit,' she admits. All her signature porcelain pieces bear several layers of meaning: a whimsical dimension (playful little characters adorn each piece); an emotive aspect (the main character often appears to be a sweet little girl); and practical attributes (each of the functional pieces relates to the others, and together the collection forms a harmonious, utilitarian whole).

Nathalie always prepares a sketch before embarking on the three-dimensional production phase, and for this reason always keeps a notebook with her, filled with inspired ideas. She envisages her creations as sculptures that one should look at from all angles. This confers a certain ceremonial quality on the collection. For important occasions, large plates, sweet dishes and flasks can be displayed for everyone to admire. While the use of her heroine – a woman disguised as a little girl – is a constant, Nathalie's sources of inspiration are varied. She is fascinated by the graphic aspect of plants, by the peculiarity of light filtering through clouds, the rhythmic sound of rain and all kinds of creepy-crawly or little creature. Childhood fantasies, gentle hybrids and lovely floral patterns adorn novel and generous shapes. It is only natural to long to be part of this peaceful world, and we can only imagine the happiness that Nathalie's guests must experience when they are immersed in this enchanting realm for one of her no-doubt wonderful dinner parties.

See also p. 260
www.nathaliechoux.com

1 Nathalie Choux's trademark 'woman disguised as a little girl' is used in all kinds of whimsical situations. On this charming 'Circus' plate she can be seen performing a stunt.

2 In 'Nageuse', the character stares at her gigantic distorted reflection on what appears to be the surface of water, as she is about to jump in for a swim.

3 In the studio: Nathalie has just finished painting a large plate.

4 'Sur les Nuages', a hymn to feeling liberated and free.

5 A newly completed black-and-white porcelain series. Little details, such as the girl's protruding nose, add unexpected texture and, above all, adorableness.

Nic Webb

UK

Great artisanship comes from dedication to and reverence for a chosen material. Ceramicists love porcelain, paper sculptors worship vellum, and naturally a woodcarver treasures wood, a living material with an inherent pliability. Nic Webb, whose utensils are handcrafted using traditional tools and techniques, 'to minimize the impact of my making', is a true master. An object as utilitarian as a spoon would scarcely attract our attention if it were not for Nic's talent and vision, but he is a staunch defender: 'The spoon is an ancient tool that is recognized and has its place within every culture. It is an object that serves us every day, a symbol of nourishment and hope.' Currently working in London, within a community of artists and makers at Vanguard Court Studios in Camberwell, Nic is passionate about his craft and the possibility of sourcing his favourite material ethically and sustainably. 'I love to work with green wood [fresh, living wood] because of its malleability,' he says. 'It can twist and move in the process of seasoning, creating wonderful natural surprises and allowing great freedom in my making.' Nic obtains much of his raw material from working in London's parks and gardens, though he also collects timber from all over the UK; in addition, friends bring him fine examples from all over the world. 'When I begin carving,' he says, 'I look for the differing qualities in each piece, allowing the grain and character to influence the design. Each spoon or bowl evolves to have its own personality, and, when finished, becomes a showcase for the limitless beauty of wood.' On occasion Nic also works with combinations of precious metals, ceramics and stone. 'I intend to pursue an organic approach to making,' he states, 'allowing my materials to suggest both form and narrative.' While enjoying all aspects of the making process, Nic ultimately finds most rewarding the pleasure of seeing and handling the finished objects. He explores themes of germination and decay, creating objects that appear not so much to have been made by hand as to have grown or been formed by processes of natural erosion: Nic Webb as the right hand of nature.

See also p. 296
www.nicwebb.com

1

1 A masterful transformation
   is suggested by this beautiful
   juxtaposition of a twig and a
   beech 'Serving Spoon'.

2 A carpet of sawdust cushions
   curvy, feminine serving
   spoons fashioned with the
   use of sturdy carving tools.

3 Wood is everywhere in Nic
   Webb's workshop – as raw
   commodity and as finished
   item.

4 Nic's passion is a productive
   one: hundreds of carved
   pieces are shaped by his
   hands.

6

5   The warm tones of the
    various types of wood
    complement each other
    in this glorious pile-up of
    utensils and bowls.

6   This 'Eucalyptus Nut Pig'
    bowl looks as if it could have
    been found in nature, but
    it is the magical product of
    Nic's craft.

Ninainvorm

NETHERLANDS

Nina van de Goor hardly ever works with strict schedules, designs or plans. She is more spontaneous than that. Late one night, she might sit down in her studio in the Netherlands, wait to see what comes to her mind and hands, and then work frenziedly until dawn. Nina screenprints on paper and fabric, but her first love is ceramics, which she slipcasts herself. For years she simply collected mid-century modern ceramics and tableware until one day she realized she could create her own designs. She also redecorates vintage pieces of crockery by screenprinting fanciful images onto them. She is inspired by the shapes, patterns and colours of recycled items, and the opportunity they offer to combine old shapes with new touches. 'I'm pretty bad at repeating myself,' she says, 'so even if I work in series or really like a certain pattern or design, I always try to find ways to keep varying it so that no two items will ever be the same.' Nina shares an ever-changing, ever-expanding house/studio with her boyfriend, a documentary filmmaker. It is filled with her favourite vintage finds, quirky design pieces and handmade treasures, to the point that it can sometimes 'drive my boyfriend slightly

crazy', she laughs. Nina's colourful and playful creations counterbalance another more rational interest of hers: completing her final university thesis in social sciences. 'I never really wanted to become an "artist",' she says, 'and I still don't feel fully comfortable being called one. However, I find the creative work matches my personality pretty well. I like to do things my own way, with a lot of freedom and constant variation. I have a hard time disciplining myself when I'm not doing something that's really meaningful to me, but I find I can work very hard on something that really gets me going. Somehow creating has an intrinsic meaning for me that I hardly ever find in regular jobs.' Her aesthetics draw on optimism and joy. Her vases burst with colour; her plates marry vintage floral patterns with cheeky dresses and intricate rosettes; little stylish birds watch over teapots. All this makes for an enchanting creative scene, as if a twenty-first-century Alice in Wonderland had just left the room and her tea-party set behind.

See also p. 304
http://ninainvorm.punt.nl

1 Nina van de Goor's signature designs printed on paper, which she snips out to create new patterns to place on porcelain wares or stationery.

2 Collage is one of Nina's principal techniques: when applied to stationery, it offers a joyful immersion into a worry-free childhood bubble.

3 Nina's playful and whimsical style in the service of illustrative works.

4 This porcelain apple pot seems to have come straight out of a fantastical fun fair.

5 Nina favours both vintage tableware revamped with colourful collages and her own slip-cast creations combining dainty shapes and contemporary imagery.

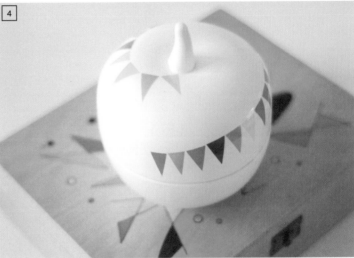

Nora Rochel

GERMANY

If there was ever a degree in the 'biology of goldsmithing', then German jewelry designer Nora Rochel would graduate with honours. One of her recent works is named after a word invented by ethnologist Irenaeus Eibl-Eisfeld: 'phytophilia', or 'the love of plants'. Nora explores flowers and organic growths as visual forms and uses them as sources of expression in her jewelry and other creations. While flowers are often associated with sentimentality, Nora takes inspiration from the full spectrum of their complexity and variety. This means that her creations exude a luxurious sophistication, and somehow any notion of flowers being merely 'pretty' is dispelled. To wear Nora's silver, gold or bronze rings, necklaces or bracelets is to turn a limb into a little landscape; a portable garden with secret retreats and niches. Many of her pieces are fanciful, but equally often the source of inspiration can be found in nature's most iconic designs – think of a pine cone, a branch of coral, a sea urchin. Nora's vivid imagination and meticulous hands enhance the initial organic shape by expanding on its most mesmerising aspects, thereby attaining the full potential of blooming beauty. Characteristic features include hidden details, such as tiny flowers located on the inside of a floral piece, or different kinds of metals used within a single object. Brightly coloured beads and stones are also precisely positioned in order to instil a dose of preciousness and to strengthen the appeal of certain pieces. Nora's creations catch the essence of nature's pure vitality but avoid the kitsch. Her porcelain vases are also inspired by flowers, though in a more abstract way. Through exuberant colours and organic shapes, they reflect the essence of flowers, here wittily growing together and epitomizing fertility and life. 'Using variously coloured porcelain slips,' she explains, 'I intuitively and spontaneously mix them in the casting process to achieve geometric, striped, dotted or marbled patterns.' Rich surface textures – resulting from textured casting forms or the application of coloured slip with a pastry bag – round out Nora's new and visceral approach to this most traditional of materials and typology. The marvels of life and the miracles of growth are clearly made visible in the positive symbolism of her creations. The outcome is a series of full-bodied, vibrant and almost living designs; extraordinary hybrids that seem to have escaped from some exotic nirvana.

See also pp. 259, 276
www.nora-rochel.de

1 Nora Rochel using a hand-tool to smoothe the inside of a bracelet in the finishing phase of production.

2 Nature is a major source of inspiration, as in this bracelet, a sea-urchin hybrid composition in brass.

3 A 925-silver ring in the form of a viral bloom of precious flowers, whose stigmas include a sapphire, a ruby, an emerald and a freshwater pearl.

4 This 925-silver ring, 'Secret Garden I', encloses a miniature floral wonderland that attests to Nora's master goldsmithing skills.

5 The lushness of this 925-silver neckpiece, 'Phytophilia', contrasts with the choice of black and the wide chain links conveying the impression of ancient alchemy.

3

5

4

6 Like protruding whipped cream cones, coloured porcelain elements adorn a pot that has been glazed on the inside.

7 A homage to sea coral: a coloured porcelain vase glazed on the inside.

6

7

Paula Juchem
ITALY

'My lines are never straight, nothing is symmetrical, and everything is about colour. It's a very Brazilian style,' says Paula Juchem. Having studied industrial design in her hometown of Santa Maria, Paula moved to Italy, where she now lives and works just outside Milan. 'My family is my greatest inspiration,' says the mother of two. 'Much of my work comes from requests from my son, Pedro. We draw together a lot. He'll ask me to draw a shark, and I'll try, and that's how it all begins.' Paula's more grown-up work, meanwhile, is driven by a flamboyant collection of females – all of whom, she says, are alternative, other-life Paulas. 'I was such a tomboy when I was little. I used to pretend I was my older brother, Luciano. I dressed like a boy. I was good at football. And so my masculine childhood has deeply influenced the fanciful women of my work. They are all "forgotten" Paulas. It is my own form of therapy!' In addition to carrying out her personal work, Paula has collaborated with many leading brands in the development of new products and innovative graphics. Commissions include illustration work for the 'Cassina LC2 Le Corbusier' project, 'Coco' wall plates for Non Sans Raison Limoges porcelain, and a panel series for the windows of the flagship Conran stores in London,

Paris and New York. Each collaboration is a joyful experience, especially the 'Monaloca' paint range she works on with Brazilian designer Elisa von Randow. 'Every time Elisa and I meet,' muses Paula, 'be it in Paris, Bahia, Milan, Torino or Venice, we embark on a three- or four-day painting marathon, working on white canvases. Once the artwork is completed, the best part is to go around the city we're in and shoot our work in some beautiful location, even in places where it's not allowed.' Other projects are testimony to her eclectic fields of creation: a collaboration with Ceramica del Ferlaro, a small porcelain company in Parma, for which she was asked to distill 'oxygen and modernity in their collection' (intriguingly, she says, 'I am working handmade tiles and three-dimensional chickens for them'). She also provided delightful illustration work for an Italian documentary, 'Divine', by Chiara Brambilla. Paula's vibrant, buoyant and semi-naïve graphic art is a breath of fresh air. Inspired by rich memories of a colourful upbringing, it instantly animates any surface. It is music to the eye.

See also p. 258
www.paulajuchem.com

1, 2 & 3 The small porcelain company Ceramica del Ferlaro commissioned Paula Juchem to introduce her style and bold modernity to their ceramics collection. Bright colours, vivid characters and a touch of humour predominate.

4 A striking face, 'Gente Strana', watches over your shoulder while you wash your hands. An Italian bathroom furniture catalogue commissioned Paula to create a tiled wall panel for this shoot.

5 Paula contributed to Chiara Brambilla's documentary, 'Divine', by illustrating the movie poster.

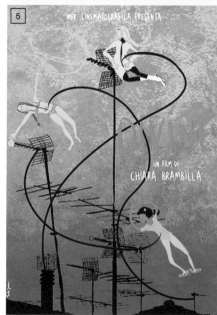

Paula Juchem

6

6 If you want something done, do it yourself: Paula is seen here finishing a tiled wall panel for her own home.

7 Enjoy a Brazilian beach wherever you are: window panel commissioned for Conran shops in London, Paris and New York.

7

8

9

8 & 10 Chicken on a plate: in order to promote the Limoges porcelain tradition, French company Non Sans Raison commissioned Paula to create a utilitarian yet funky plate set, the 'Coco' project.

9 'Monaloca', a joint project by Paula Juchem and Brazil-based art director Elisa von Randow. Taking inspiration from locations in and photographs of Italy and Brazil, they created vibrant cotton bedcovers with imagery aimed to promote freedom of sexual preference.

Puddin'head

AUSTRALIA

From early cartographers' descriptions of the New World and its fantastic creatures to the Surrealist movement's exploration of the subconscious imagination, Richard McAdam's sources of inspiration are diverse. He finds himself drawn to European folktales and their powerful, often dark narratives and characters, and also to outsider art and children's drawings for their honest, often untrained techniques. If there is an underlying thread in his work, it is a gentle humour that is more whimsical than hard-edged. Based in Sydney, Richard surrounds himself with as many books as he can. 'Libraries are such an exciting place for me,' he confides, 'and the larger and dustier they are, the better. I scour every kind of source material for a phrase or illustration that might set off my imagination and find its way into my designs.' Richard has been drawing for as long as he can remember. He always loved illustrating stories he had read, making up characters and settings for them. 'Thankfully I came from a family that understood my need to create, and they actively encouraged me to continue and pursue my passion. At art school I was awakened to the joys

and heartaches of printmaking, the exacting nature of editions, and most of all the power of negative space within an image and on the page.' The logical step for Richard was to make his designs accessible to a broader audience than a gallery context generally allows. And so Puddin'head was born. Richard finds the utilitarian aspect to his collection 'pleasing', the fine-art canvas being replaced by linen, including a range of tea towels. Wall pieces are printed on Belgian linen and hand-embroidered, a process he finds laborious yet 'therapeutic'. 'I like the shot of intense colour that the embroidery brings to these works,' he adds. 'My pieces are made with such love and attention to detail that just would not be there in a mechanized process. As a result, I think there's an integrity in my work.' A proud stag strikes a pose, flaunting its rose-adorned crown of antlers, and an elephant trumpets out a plush bunch of flowers: two blissful and extraordinary sights that can now be enjoyed every day.

See also p. 306
www.puddinhead.com.au

1 The animal kingdom as source of inspiration: a combination of montage, drawing and painting to achieve the final design.

2 Each Puddin'head creation is delivered with a signature swing tag featuring a stag with flowers sprouting from its antlers.

3 Puddin'head's tea towels are carefully packaged in a printed cardboard envelope detailing the design and colour scheme of the contents.

4 During the screenprinting stage for this 'Poppy' design, a floodbar is used to fill the stencil openings with bright red ink.

5 The star line-up! 'Antlers' tea towels are left to dry after being printed.

6 Richard McAdam also produces purely artistic works, as shown in this detail of hand-printed, hand-embroidered artwork on Belgian linen.

Rohan Eason

UK

Rohan Eason has always drawn and experimented with new processes and techniques. 'Painting was my first love,' he says, 'and formed the grounding to all of my professional practice, whether making fabric prints or illustrations for books. I spent my youth surrounded by artists – my mother and father, sister, grandfather and uncle have all pursued the arts – and for this reason I enjoyed a very colourful and engaging time as a child.' Rohan craves the illustration of the human form in all of its intricacies and nuances: the face, the character, the emotions, elements that a photograph can capture for a moment but that a painting can hold organically and richly forever, 'for it holds the essence of the maker and their thoughts, too'. Rohan's work begins with nature, and research is the most important stage of any of his projects. He finds visits to the many libraries of London extremely helpful in gaining knowledge of a subject, but real life and the natural environment are still his favourite sources of inspiration. 'It's so compelling to look to the wonder of the world that surrounds us,' he says. 'I love to get out of my studio and wander the streets, visit the parks and city, capturing ideas and moments for later use. Once I have enough resources, I venture back to my nest. I look for patterns, I pull out some kind of ordered chaos, so prevalent in nature, and I try to recreate this in a very organized way. I pursue a perfection of line, a balance of block, pattern and space.' Rohan believes that a good image can captivate the viewer, trapping them in a mesmerising circle of beauty and fascination, or horror and controversy. His work is not always easy to view – the darkness in some of the words he has illustrated can be said to suit his style even more than the light – but, through unbroken lines and intricate patterns, he hopes to impel the viewer ever deeper into his work. He is also keen to develop and diversify. 'My current engagement is colour,' he states. 'Something I've handled alone but never in conjunction with the black-and-white work I'm better known for. This is my new excitement, my new challenge, my new adventure.' It will be ours, too.

See also p. 249
www.rohaneason.com

1 Illustration in the service of fashion: the white leather jacket of a private client has been embellished with a tattoo-like, pen-drawn goddess.

2 Full concentration required: the artist at work in his studio.

3 'The Circle', an enchanting though rather ominous black-and-white illustration, commissioned for the children's book *Anna & the Witch's Bottle* by Geoff Cox, published by Black Maps Press.

Rothschild & Bickers

UK

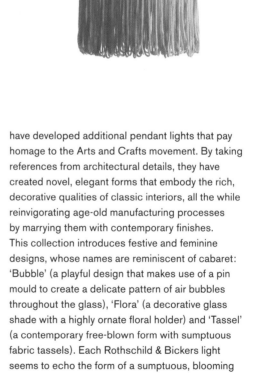

Here comes the light! English glass artisans Victoria Rothschild and Mark Bickers combine traditional techniques with cutting-edge design. All of their works are made at the London Glassworks workshop and use free-blown glass for optimum quality. The workshop is one of the last in the UK and strives to promote superior craftsmanship. Rothschild & Bickers specialize in creating unique bespoke glass for lighting and interior products. Together, Victoria and Mark have over twenty years' experience in working glass, which gives them an extensive knowledge of many techniques, including lampworking, sandblasting, polishing, etching, mirroring, cutting and kiln-forming. Their signature collection is rich with luscious designs. The 'Spindle' shade and pendant combine the rich texture of hand-blown glass with the subtle intricacy of lamp-worked borosilicate. The 'Lantern Light' embodies the pure elegance and simplicity of handmade glass by harnessing its natural fluidity: during the making process, the duo skilfully allow the glass to stretch while it is being blown into its final shape. The classically shaped 'Open Optic' has a delicate scalloped rim, which looks wonderful at a low height; the 'Opulent Optic' combines classic form and vibrant colour to infuse an oriental flavour. The 'Black Nouveau' range, meanwhile, is made using traditional free-blown techniques to create graceful forms with a shiny, reflective quality. Last but not least, the 'Vintage Light', a flamboyant light with a lavish cascade of fringing, conveys a sense of antique grandeur. Hoping to build on the success of this comprehensive core range, Rothschild & Bickers

have developed additional pendant lights that pay homage to the Arts and Crafts movement. By taking references from architectural details, they have created novel, elegant forms that embody the rich, decorative qualities of classic interiors, all the while reinvigorating age-old manufacturing processes by marrying them with contemporary finishes. This collection introduces festive and feminine designs, whose names are reminiscent of cabaret: 'Bubble' (a playful design that makes use of a pin mould to create a delicate pattern of air bubbles throughout the glass), 'Flora' (a decorative glass shade with a highly ornate floral holder) and 'Tassel' (a contemporary free-blown form with sumptuous fabric tassels). Each Rothschild & Bickers light seems to echo the form of a sumptuous, blooming flower: indeed, this talented duo could be described as 'glass horticulturists'.

See also p. 289
www.rothschildbickers.com

1 The optical glass of this hand-blown, fabric-trimmed bronze 'Opulent Optic' refracts light and emanates diffuse coloured shadows throughout a room.

2 Gathering glass from the furnace on the end of a blowing iron.

3 Reheating glass in the glory hole gas-fired chamber.

4

4 'Flora Pendant', a small hand-blown glass shade, with elaborate pressed-metal holder, looks like an elegant ripe fruit.

5 One of the last free-blown glass workshops in the UK: a vast space in which traditional and cutting-edge approaches coexist.

6 Inspired by Victorian decadence, the 'Tassel Light' is a versatile piece that can adorn either a contemporary or a period setting.

7 The gently scalloped rim of the 'Open Optic' has a feminine quality, like the frail petals of a petunia or the flowing hem of a dress.

8 Opening the lehr, a kiln for annealing glass and cooling it overnight at a regulated heat to prevent cracking.

9 Teamwork: an assistant gives a bench blow while the master shapes the form with a damp paper pad.

5

6

7

8

9

Sarah Cihat

USA

Challenging what she calls the 'commercial culture of buy, buy; throw it away; get the next new thing', Sarah Cihat hand-selects used or unwanted ceramics from Goodwill and Salvation Army outposts and retail-store reject piles, then cleans and transforms them by redesigning and resurfacing them. This is the basis of her 'Rehabilitated Dishware' collection. 'There are perfectly good dishes in thrift stores that no one wants,' she points out. 'When I see stacks with really hideous designs, I think, "What could they become?"' Originally from Cookeville, Tennessee, Sarah attended the Parsons School of Design in New York, where she graduated in product design and developed the rehabilitation concept as part of her thesis. From galloping horse silhouettes through floating florals to presidential profiles, Sarah produces striking, unpretentious images that transcend trends. Her contemporary patterns and vivid palettes transform discarded items into unique keepsakes. She has also expanded her portfolio to include the 'Dirt' collection, experimenting with slipcast porcelain pieces featuring relief, under-glazing, stunning decals and original elegant shapes with a twist. 'I find balance and movement in asymmetry,' says Sarah. 'The faceted surfaces of some of my work I find through working with moist clay to make a shape. Just through playing with it, and pounding and hitting it, a shape begins to take form. From there, I manipulate, chisel and sand my way to a pattern or surface that pleases me. I like to think of them as little messed-up diamonds or strange rocks.' Sarah also co-designs, with Frederick Bouchardy of fragrance brand Joya, a range of perfumes, soap sets, scented candles and oil diffusers. In addition, she collaborates with metalsmith Michael Miller on a range of porcelain bowls with chains. This collection, called 'Taken', is a highly successful combination of clay and metal, the different elements of each maker's craft. Sarah is not interested in creating fragile 'art', nor does she wish to preach about green issues, though she acknowledges, 'I want my work to be something that people want to keep for a long time and not throw out.' Desirable creations that last: what better way to a sustainable future?

See also pp. 264, 305
www.sarahcihat.com

1 Sarah Cihat teamed up with Joya founder Frederick Bouchardy to create the hand-cast porcelain perfume bottles for Joya's avant-garde fragrance 'FvsS: Parfums'.

2 Sarah uses a soft sanding pad to clean delicate porcelain greenware perfume bottles and wands from the 'FvsS' collection before high-firing them in the kiln.

3 Each perfume bottle lid has a long wand that can reach deep into the exquisite scent.

4 The fired wands are hand-painted with 22-carat gold to add an extra hidden precious touch before the pieces are fired for the second time at a much lower temperature.

1

5

6

7

8

5 & 6 Combining flora and fauna silhouettes, the 'Rehabilitated', or 'Rehab', series is a project that upcycles old plates with a modern and vibrant twist. 'Turquoise Horse No. 2' and 'Lime Doe No. 3' are fine examples.

7 Cleaning up the glaze on a dinner plate from the 'Rehabilitated Dishware' line before firing.

8 Stacks of used dishes will receive a stencil, get reglazed and then fired for the 'Rehabilitated Dishware' line.

9

9 The call of the wild: a white porcelain 'Wolf with Dogwood Flowers' from the 'Dirt' collection.

Serrote

PORTUGAL

When an old technique is at risk of being lost, it is always uplifting to find that there are enthusiastic individuals who will take up the trade from scratch, bringing a formerly mainstream method back to its glory days, and, by updating what can be done with it, making it desirable again, thus securing its future. This is exactly what a Portuguese couple from Lisbon have accomplished. After several years of teaching and web designing, Nuno Neves and Susana Vilela embarked upon a personal journey – a project that aimed to use letterpress machinery to create a stationery line, which, while contemporary, was anchored in the past. The couple were familiar with the technology but they hadn't had the opportunity to use it, and, since letterpress devices were becoming increasingly rare, time was running out. After a good deal of searching, they found a few traditional printers tucked away in the old neighbourhoods of Lisbon, where typesetters were still printing invoices and business cards the old way. And so Serrote was born. Their sources of inspiration are many: trips around Portugal, comics and pixel-art artists, and above all, the prolific work of all the anonymous graphic artists who once

designed packaging for everyday Portuguese objects (tuna fish cans, toothpaste boxes, soaps, candy bags, traffic signs and store signs, to name but a few). So Nuno and Susana embarked on their first project, a notebook, for which they used old metal types and ornaments. They found these traditional tools, long untouched, by literally delving into ancient typesetting drawers. Their first notebook, titled 'Plain', had a unique and appealing two-tone cover. Nuno and Susana quickly set up a website to promote their creation. The feedback was immediately encouraging. The Serrote duo decided next to produce a 'Squared' notebook, and soon after a third one, numbered and in limited edition, filled with vellum paper. The stationery collection expanded quickly, and the print run increased hugely. Serrote's most popular product is now the 'Toalha de Mesa', a notebook filled with the traditional tablecloth paper used in Portuguese restaurants, which has a pleasing texture and is used for scribbling on after meals.

See also pp. 1, 299
www.serrote.com

1 A vintage letterpress at the ready.

2 The cover of the 'Vellum Paper' notebook goes through its first press.

3 Serrote's 'Plain Paper' and 'Squared Paper' notebooks were printed using the Gutenberg method in an old-fashioned printing factory.

4 The finished cover of the 'Vellum Paper' notebook is printed in letterpress with metal figures and wooden type.

5 The Saxicola torquata, or Stonechat bird, is part of the 'Três Passaros' ('Three Birds') artwork, made as a limited-edition numbered print with chlorine- and acid-free cotton paper.

3

4

5

Saxicola torquata

Severija Inčirauskaitė-Kriaunevičienė

LITHUANIA

1 As this artwork from the 'Way of Roses' series shows, car hoods make the perfect sturdy canvases for extraordinary cross-stitched floral designs.

2 Holes are drilled according to a pre-set pattern. These will later be cross-stitched by hand with cotton threads.

3 Beauty and the beast: a 'Way of Roses' series artwork beautifying an old car door.

4 The rustier the better, and a dose of humour for these sunny-side-up eggs on a pan from the 'Autumn Collection' series.

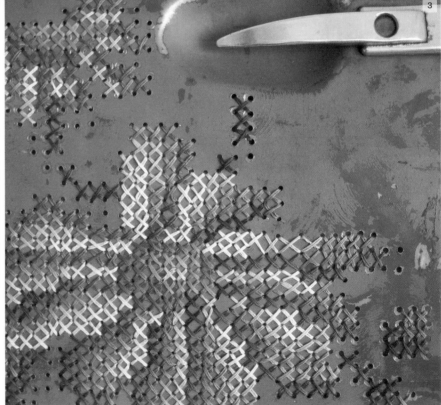

The stunning contrast between rusty metal and pretty cross-stitch is a testament to Severija Inčirauskaitė-Kriaunevičienė's artistic talent and cultural heritage. Her parents were both artists and associate professors at the VAA Telšiai Faculty of Arts, and so Severija was exposed to art from a young age. She rapidly developed an interest in metal, for its sturdiness, weight and malleability, but she was also drawn to textiles, for their softness. She now experiments with these two materials, and they have come to define her vision. She likes to choose everyday, utilitarian metal objects as the 'heroes' of her works; objects that evoke comfort and routine. Once adorned with embroidery, they start to remind us of the craft souvenirs that the general public likes to collect in order to create a nostalgic environment that is familiar and restful. 'Kitsch' is the obvious notion associated with this tendency; a concept that Severija both embraces and validates. 'In my work, I take pleasure in things that are only insignificant details to most people,' she says. 'An ordinary human being and the mundane fragments of his or her life acquire an exceptionally important meaning in my work.' Severija is driven by an inherent understanding

of the beauty that can be found in the banal. She often uses a simple language of symbols: flowers stand for beauty; lids, buckets, watering cans and shredders relate to the domestic, material side of life. Her usage of the age-old technique of cross-stitch could be taken as a reference to the stereotypically tasteless, twee form of the embroidery, but by choosing this specific technique and by combining it with 'syrupy' fragments of popular culture in order to transform her objects into aesthetic creations, Severija raises doubts as to the traditional hierarchy of art; what is usually called 'high art' and what is perceived as less valuable. 'In my works, the kitsch details of popular culture lose their clearly negative connotation. A simple understanding of beauty characteristic to ordinary people can also be valuable because it is part of life, and sincere,' she explains. By a creative reversal of fortune, the mundane becomes desirable and the ordinary exceptional. Severija's decision to marry metal with stitching is an exhibition of artistic prowess, and a true homage to her Lithuanian roots.

See also p. 253
www.severija.lt

Sia Mai

DENMARK

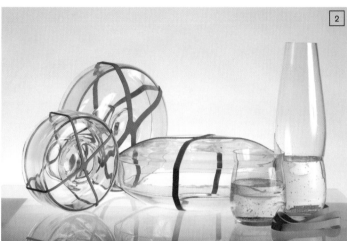

4

5

Benefiting from the best of both worlds, Sia Mai divides her time between her native Denmark and neighbouring Sweden, where she lives. 'Denmark is dominated by studio glass and art glass, whereas Sweden is associated with glass as an industry,' she notes. Thus she commutes between Copenhagen, which is a significant market for her, and the deep woods of Sweden, where her glass is produced in small factories. 'I work closely with the master blowers,' she says, 'physically participating in the making of my glass.' Since graduating from the Danish Design School, Sia has had many exhibitions and taken part in many 'Danish Crafts Collection' fairs; finished pieces have also been displayed at the Ebeltoft Glass Museum. When creating, she first uses clay or plaster moulds, as these enable her to draft her ideas and determine the scale of her pieces. Her prototypes can then be quickly and easily translated into finished glass products. Common characteristics are the ways in which her shapes fit together and the surprising number of their utilitarian functions. In her work, Sia explores the various types of glass container commonly used for storing foodstuffs and beverages. She strives to turn our daily mealtimes into inspiring sensory experiences by adapting the original idea of glass storage to our modern way of life. The serving vessels in her 'Picnic' range might well inspire us to stage a picnic in our own living room; as reinterpretations of familiar icons, such as the lunch box and the canteen flask, they draw attention to the profound changes in our everyday lifestyle. Her elegant 'Drinking Glass' series is made from thin glass that condenses colour, making the pieces seem almost invisible. Her 'Carafe with Lid' was developed as part of a series of containers for the refrigerator: both the carafe and its lid are made from clear glass, which allows the attributes of the material to be experienced as the solid lid and the blown bottle come together. 'Glass is transparent, and its surface is smooth and clean, which makes it very useful for meals and cooking, as it's very hygienic. I never get tired of making new bottles and watching the colour of drinks interact with the optics of the glass,' Sia enthuses. When utility meets refinement, and clever design meets expert craft, miracles can certainly happen around the dining table.

1 Have you ever looked through a rainbow? The 'Drinking Glass' series offers the experience thanks to its dense colour hues and transparent thinness.

2 Reinventing picnic wares, the clear 'Picnic' collection is functional, hygienic and beautiful to live with.

3 The 'Picnic' series also comes in various colours. The glossy chromatic aspect is enough to make anyone's mouth water.

4 The production leftovers from the 'Structure' glass series form a beautiful entity all by themselves.

5 Blowing a 'Structure' carafe, a meticulous piece of teamwork.

See also p. 271
www.siamai.dk

Siba Sahabi

NETHERLANDS

'What fascinates me about paper is its fragile, transient quality. My delicate but pliant objects come into being through a slow process. I try not to focus only on the result but also on the process. For me it's important to forge an emotional bond between me, the human being, and the paper that is taking shape in my hands.' The daughter of a German mother and an Iranian father, Siba Sahabi designs paper objects in her studio in Amsterdam. Inspired by the history of Middle Eastern tableware, she aims to build a bridge between the Orient and the Occident, conveying how the two cultures influence one another, leading to renewal and cultural richness. 'I want to emphasize the ongoing importance of cultural melting pots,' she declares. Recapturing traces of the past that have got lost in time and space is her drive. Siba redefines the meaning of these fragments of an earlier era by linking them to contemporary design. 'Bucchero' is a series of paper vessels that takes inspiration directly from traditional black Etruscan ceramics. It consists of several pieces – carafes, goblets and cups – that are handcrafted from black wallpaper used for its strength and its resistance to light. Another series, 'Tea Dance', was inspired by the journey of tea from the East to the West. In polite Moroccan society, ladies were asked to perform dances to amuse guests who had been invited for tea; French colonial families adopted the idea, and a gentle waltz around the tea table became the fashion. The 'Tea Dance' collection is about paper teapots and glasses performing their own delicate dance. All Siba's pieces are made out of paper strips, using a slow and rhythmic technique that involves cutting, folding, rolling and gluing. This ensures a visual sense of movement, for Siba is interested in adding a third dimension to the humble, flat material that is paper. The result has similarities to ceramics produced on a potter's wheel: a circular body around a vertical axis, with fine horizontal striations. Siba's unique ability to sculpt delicate and meaningful vessels out of paper has earned her much acclaim, including first prize at the Comeseedo competition in Berlin and the Most Remarkable Repair Award from Amsterdam's Platform21. She has 'translated culture into objects', and the results are beautiful.

See also p. 295
www.sibasahabi.com

1 & 2 Siba Sahabi building the base of a paper vessel – fine strips of paper rolled and glued together – in her bright studio, highly representative of her clean, elegant creations.

3 & 4 The 'Tea Dance' series is an invitation to travel and participate in an imaginary North African tea ceremony. The fine design of the teapots and tumblers is reminiscent of the sophistication and style of Arabic art.

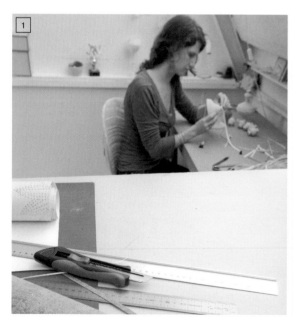

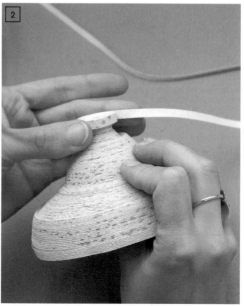

6

5 & 6 These 'Bucchero'
sculptures – made with
Siba's signature circular
paper-strip technique –
perfectly exemplify their
black Etruscan heritage,
giving the impression
that they are part of a rare
archaeological hoard.

Silke Decker

GERMANY

At the core of a fine vessel is a superb geometrical web. By a magical twist, threads seem to hold themselves up and float. Silke Decker's 'cord' technique dissolves the classic exterior of tableware and exposes its lace-like skeleton … and thus a filigree structure of seemingly fragile but nevertheless sturdy porcelain comes into being. The function of the vessel becomes utilitarian, but as a decorative object it holds the aesthetic value that is inherently attached to a work of art. Of her process, Silke says: 'I have always liked to create something with my hands, to see it grow, change and sometimes turn out differently than planned. Usually I start by taking inspiration from a structure that exists in nature, maths, art, textiles or craftwork, and then patiently I observe how it develops.' She is a product designer who takes great satisfaction in immersing herself in her latest artistic project. 'It's like taking a break, a moment, for new impulses and directions. It recalls when I was a child and my main leisure activity was to paint, glue or create something,' she muses. During her study of industrial design, Silke took a class in ceramics and soon discovered the joy of experimenting with surfaces, dipping all kinds of materials, including paper, foam, moss, grass and threads, into liquid

porcelain. She has never looked back, and today continues to explore her 'self-inspired' technique. During an exhibition while she was at university, she met businessman and ceramic collector Peter Siemssen, who invited her to take up a scholarship from his foundation. At this point her 'cord' creations became more functional, and her concept of 'cordporcelain' was realized. This defining collaboration has been tremendously fruitful; years later, Silke is warmly accepted as a permanent guest in the studio. 'Porcelain as a material is fascinating; the way clay can metamorphose into something hard, durable and lustrous following its own dictum. I never tire of working the clay until it's at its best,' she states. In creating intricate, 'ossified' objects, Silke redefines the common perception of porcelain. Here the physical structure takes centre stage, and puts itself firmly in the contemporary arena.

See also p. 255
www.silkedecker.de

1 The wet woollen threads of a 'cordporcelain' bowl, seen here on their plaster mould. The various colours will turn to white during the firing process.

2 In the workshop of the Peter Siemssen Foundation, Silke Decker places wet woollen threads following a precise pattern that will form a bowl.

3 Silke uses a brush to clean the rim of a bowl at the Pierre Arquié porcelain factory in Limoges, France.

4 The random woven aspect of this cordporcelain bowl from the 'Classic Pattern' collection captures the essence of a light bird's nest.

5 The two-toned threads of this cordporcelain bowl lend a sophisticated and complex look to the object, as if it has been engineered by an ingenious spider.

4

5

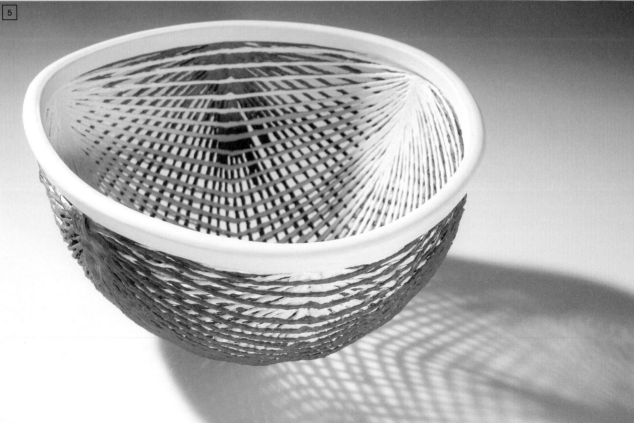

6

7

6 A light brushstroke of pure gold adorns these cordporcelain bowls from the 'Framework Pattern' collection; part origami-like constructions, part modular hemispheres.

7 A brown and white cordporcelain plate appears to float, its intricately woven body reminiscent of rich textiles.

Sissel Wathne

DENMARK

Have you noticed what is happening? Look a little closer. An urban invasion of porcelain objects and characters has infiltrated the city. Static streams of brown clay or a white substance issue out of drainpipes and gutters. A sweet little winter doe sits peacefully on a public bench, and it looks as if his miniature surroundings – delicate trees sprouting out of the snowfall – have followed him. This subtle community-metamorphosis is the collaborative work of two talented ceramicists, Norwegian Sigrid Espelien and Danish Sissel Wathne. Sissel, born and raised in the small town of Gilleleje, grew up accompanying her grandmother – also a ceramicist – to the local evening school when her grandmother held ceramics classes. Sissel was inspired for life. She passed her first art course at the age of 17, and has not strayed from clay ever since. 'I have an indescribable passion for my subject and material, and cannot imagine a second career,' she enthuses, 'and I could not live without creating with ceramics.' She studied ceramics as an exchange student in Pennsylvania, USA, at several Danish schools, including the Svendborg School of Arts, the Aarhus Academy of Arts, and the Glass and Ceramic School at Bornholm, and latterly at the Royal College of Art in London. 'Work originates from my curiosity with visual communication,' she says. 'I explore and experiment with the possibilities that lie in using ceramics as a narrative medium.' During her creative processes, Sissel focuses on thoughts and ideas, not just shapes. Take her 'Mrs Ingeborg' eggcup: a porcelain plucked chicken becomes a slightly disturbing yet appropriate receptacle for an egg. Or her 'Knitted Cylinders', whose cabled surfaces are so realistically textured that one fears they could not possibly hold any liquid. Her 'Traces of Everyday' series looks fragile and 'bruised'; we feel tenderness towards so much beautiful vulnerability on display. Sissel succeeds in her aim. Through her ceramic creations – some utilitarian and some artistic – she excites our intellect and emotions by distilling a dose of deception, mystery and humour.

See also pp. 262, 302
www.sisselwathne.com

1 Preparing hooks and white plaster streams to invade the urban landscape for the 'Street Ceramics' installation, Versterbro, Copenhagen.

2 Pallets of red earthenware bunches of grass dry before being fired and dispersed in the outside world.

3 This little pastoral scene was assembled using ready-made and modelled ceramic characters as part of the 'Animals in Landscape' series for the 'Street Ceramics' installation project.

4 The 'Things Come Out' series, from the 'Street Ceramics' project, encourages pedestrians to explore their surroundings and pay attention to spots they would normally ignore, such as pipes and cracks.

5 When mundane indoor objects are placed out of context: these little hooks from the 'Animals in Landscape' series have no proper use, and yet they can function in their new location.

Sissel Wathne

6 A public bench is occupied here by a peaceful winter scene from the 'Animals in Landscape' series.

7 A technical tour de force: the 'Knitted Cylinder' from the 'Knitted Everyday Ware' in delicate biscuit earthenware.

8 The spring flowers in this 'Flower Meadow' scene, from the 'Ceramic World – Everyday Still Life' project, originate from floral-patterned cups, cut into individual ceramic figures.

9 'Mrs Ingeborg', a quirky kitchen accessory set. Having challenged herself to slaughter four free-range fowl in the name of art, Sissel Wathne cast them in plaster, produced them in porcelain and applied gold to the egg cavity.

10 A cute tea-party scene created for the 'Ceramic World – Everyday Still Life' project: a miniature universe, a little floating island, pure visual storytelling.

Soojin Kang

UK

Crafting as an organic extension of a vintage utilitarian object; it takes the form of a stylish outgrowth, a fine mass that behaves like cotton or wool ivy, a handmade graft that expands the object so that it takes on a temporary but superior new shape. This is 'A Continuous Chain', which, along with a second project, 'Dressed Furniture', is Soojin Kang's main series. Both attempt to answer the question: how can traditional crafts be contextualized into contemporary forms? Born in Seoul, South Korea, Soojin graduated from London's Central Saint Martins College of Art and Design with a bachelor's degree in fashion design and prints, and a master's degree in textile futures. She gained experience as a design assistant and a fabric and print developer at various fashion houses. Now her creative fields of choice are textile and

furniture design. 'A Continuous Chain' has a kind of conceptual functionality, but it begs the question, is this kind of craftwork fashion, interior design, art, or possibly all three? It conveys the beauty of traditional artisanship and antique raw materials, but in a contemporary context. It also explores the emotional relationship between humans and objects. A lack of an emotional, personal bond between owners and their belongings has gradually emerged in our time and can be accounted for by the phenomenon of fast-changing trends. Against the backdrop of this new disposability, Soojin's collection aims to highlight the significance of handcraft and the added value such artisanship confers. 'Handcrafting is a slow and thoughtful process that truly engages the maker into carefully giving great attention to the product,' says Soojin. 'It's no longer a fleeting fashion item to be discarded after one season, but rather a personal story to be continued.' Indeed, none of the objects Soojin offers has reached its final state, as one can carry on building or, for that matter, unravelling her designs. Both projects make us consider our basic needs and the things we have surrounding us, and encourage us to use these things wisely and beautifully. This is precisely why Soojin has employed handcrafting as her method and vehicle, and antique raw materials as her subject. She has succeeded in re-establishing a conversation between the owner and the object; in having us care more about and develop sentiments toward handcrafted pieces. While Soojin's project may have started out as a conceptual idea, we can now see her chairs as superb additions to the home, and her watches and necklaces as unique accessories for an avant-garde wardrobe.

See also pp. 267, 278
www.soojinkang.net

1

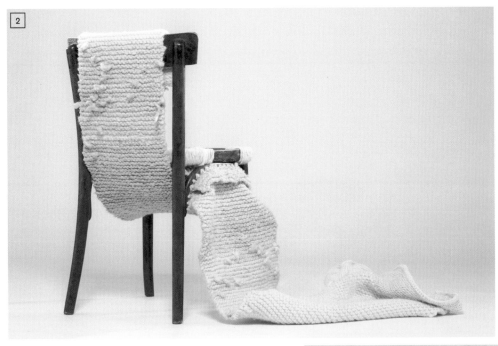

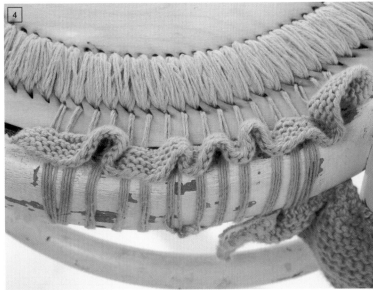

1 Detail of the 'Knitted Chair', part of Soojin Kang's 'A Continuous Chain' project: an antique chair used as a frame for a wool-knitted composition that can be perpetually extended.

2 The 'Knitted Chair' aims to highlight the significance of 'handmade': a true work in progress, an open invitation for the owner to carry on the story.

3 & 4 The frilly skirt of the 'Skirt Chair' – a flirty sister of the 'Knitted Chair' – was stitched to the base and around the legs, protruding on one side inside the space between the wooden frame and the seat.

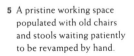

5 A pristine working space
   populated with old chairs
   and stools waiting patiently
   to be revamped by hand.

6 The 'Dressed Chair', part
   of the 'Dressed Furniture'
   project: an entire antique
   dining chair bandaged by
   hand with coloured strips
   of smooth suede, instilling
   a colour-block/patchwork
   aspect.

7 Experimental design leading
   to a new emotional aesthetic
   and an avant-garde use
   of antique objects. A ring
   and a knitted glove, part of
   Soojin's 'Wearable' collection
   of unique and meaningful
   jewelry, become extensions
   of one another.

Sophie Cook

UK

Ethereal bottles and pods on the wheel: Sophie Cook uses fluid porcelain and vibrant glazes to create subtle, sculptural ceramic ware. Each bottle or pod is left to dry overnight. It is then hand-carved to give extra definition to its form, the carving being an incredibly delicate process that inevitably results in many breakages. After a few days' drying, each piece is embossed with the initials 'SC' and bisque fired. The glaze is then applied using a spray gun and the pieces are fired to 1260°C. The apparent simplicity of Sophie's work is misleading. The glazes have taken several years of fine-tuning, and she is always seeking out new colours. She would love to be able to create a red or a strong orange, but this has proved practically impossible, as these colours burn away at such high temperatures. During the glaze firing, there are further risks due to the fragility of the porcelain and the heat of the kiln. It only takes an air bubble or an imperfection in the glaze for Sophie to discount a piece. 'I am trying to stop being such a perfectionist and just accept that every piece is unique for its own qualities,' she says, acknowledging that, 'I'm better at saying this than actually putting it into practice. The studio is full of "seconds", which I sell off at sales.' On average, during the entire making process, only fifty per cent of the pieces will make it to shops or galleries. Sophie, a graduate of Camberwell School of Arts, sells her work worldwide and it is also featured in the permanent collections of the Geffrye Museum in

London and the Manchester City Galleries. In 2009, her work was chosen to be in the European Design Show, which will become a permanent fixture in the Indianapolis Museum of Art. Her original inspiration came from an urge to react against much of the traditional ceramic work she had seen, where the glazes seemed dark and murky. 'I want to create pieces where colour embodies the pot, rather than being surface decoration,' she states. A new series involves abstract splashes of colour being turned into landscape scenes by the addition of small images of people, animals and scenery. Essence of form, simplicity, and a large and subtle colour range remain Sophie's trademarks. Her work is a collector's dream. The more you own, the better it looks.

See also pp. 3, 265
www.sophiecook.com

1 Sophie Cook turning the semi-dry pod.

2 Refining the neck of the pod with a metal kidney.

3 These workshop shelves hold an inventory of vases in all shapes and sizes – teardrop, pod and bottle; small, medium and large. Despite the overall sleek style, each is unique.

String Gardens

NETHERLANDS

1 & 2 Maintenance hub as well as production line: the workshop is the den of a genius horticulturist.

3 The sky is the limit: Jonagold apple, Gieser Wilderman pear and Amelanchier trees are bound together in a semi-permanent poetic dance.

Jasmine, clematis, passionflower, rare orchids and many other exotic and ancient plants; all these living organisms are very lucky. They can rise above it all in Fedor van der Valk's magical hands. Fedor is more than green-fingered; he is gifted with an extraordinary ability to tame Mother Nature and extract the beauty at her core. String Gardens started in 2008 as a project run by the creative collective Studio IJM. Its main objective was to bring plants to eye level. This style of hanging plant is a variation on *kokedema*, the Japanese botanical style in which plants are covered with moss and placed in a bowl. In the case of String Gardens, the plants have to find their balance while growing larger and getting heavier. The plants' centre of gravity continually changes, and consequently the plants grow in a way that makes them look powerful, as if they are floating in mid-air. Water is supplied in different ways: some plants have built-in glass reservoirs (an artificial root made of moss transports the water to the soil ball); other plants are woven into horizontal nets that are covered with moss, clover and grass, while a water-dripping system keeps everything wet. Most plants have a bath approximately every three days. 'I very much like the contrast between the dry, seemingly brittle stems and the heavy green growth, the contrast between eggshell-like thinness and the strength of the robust shape,' explains Fedor. He likes the plants to look as if they need to be constrained. 'I tie down stems and twigs so as to permanently have this "forever springtime"-feeling of bursting open,' he shares excitedly. 'It's hard to capture this in an image but, for me, most of the plants look as if they are frozen in the middle of a jump, while still growing and flowering.' Fedor's frames of reference extend widely. He is fascinated by cities that have a complicated street layout and a giant network of electricity cables hanging overhead, as in Rome or Istanbul. 'My dream would be to live in a quiet apartment, with a parlour filled with plants and overlooking moving clouds. In the meantime, I try to create a similar dimension for myself and others through String Gardens.' Among Fedor's creations, we in turn feel as if we're floating in a parallel universe, under an otherworldly canopy, where flowers, shrubs and bulbs are the living stars.

See also p. 4
www.stringgardens.com

4 A complex network of
   interconnecting cables
   gives the appropriate name
   to 'String Gardens'.

5 A regal sight: the Fritillaria
   flower in full bloom, its
   graceful stems and leaves
   sashaying up in the air.

Studio Kiki van Eijk

NETHERLANDS

5

1 Liquid clay is poured into the handmade 'Celadon Plate' mould.

2 Intriguingly, the 'Soft Teapot' appears to be padded, but it is solid porcelain merely bearing the trace of the handmaking process.

3 Cleaning the surface of the 'Soft Clock' with a sanding pad just before firing.

4 The spectacular glossy copper finish of the 'Soft Clock' after firing.

5 Reinventing traditional cutlery with this 'Silverware' line, made with porcelain and stainless steel.

Kiki van Eijk loves stories. In fact, her early sketches could easily have served to illustrate the imaginative worlds of Mary Poppins or Alice in Wonderland. Kiki graduated with honours from the Design Academy Eindhoven and, besides developing her own collection, was formerly the art director of the Academy restaurant. She has always drawn inspiration from everyday objects and small details. Thanks to her uncanny ability to spot noteworthy imagery, she operates with a 'love at first sight' technique. Her creations are all made so that people will fall in love with them, the same way she fell in love the first time she stumbled across her source of inspiration. Lately, her design process has become even more intuitive: she works from a completely blank canvas. Her many, varied creations are easily recognizable by their playful designs; her eponymous 'Kiki Carpet' is a good example. But do not be misled by your first impressions: what might initially look soft and lighthearted can actually be hard and serious in intent. Another facet of Kiki's talent is her affiliation for materials and the layers within. This aptitude results in innovative and surprising techniques being applied to an object, unexpectedly and with real craftsmanship. Making products by hand is paramount to Kiki's vision,

and it also influences her more industrial projects. Consequently, she not only challenges us, the viewers, but also the manufacturers and craftsmen who help produce her designs. Her success has meant that her collections have been shown in international galleries and museums, and have also featured in high-profile publications worldwide. Kiki regularly undertakes commissions for clients such as Studio Edelkoort Paris, MOOOI, Ahrend, Royal Leerdam Crystal, the Audax Textile Museum and the Zuiderzeemuseum Enkhuizen, to name but a few. Her nostalgic approach, combined with a poetic and intimate style, comes to life in a wide range of works, including lighting, furniture, ceramics, glassware and luxury textiles. 'In these times of quick change,' she says, 'I find it important still to stand by the everyday object that is made with love. Autonomy is very important in my work, in order to have the freedom to be as personal as I like without being distracted by customers' wishes. I choose to work not only with sustainable materials, but also with products that have an everlasting and timeless image.'

See also pp. 254, 269, 271, 287, 300, 309
www.kikiworld.nl

6

6 'Like an enormous patchwork
of ideas': 'Cut and Paste',
a furniture accessory
collaboration between Kiki
van Eijk and Secondome
director Claudia Pignatale.

7 Sketch for 'Totem', a pile-up
of cabinets and niches with
mirrors and storage, from the
'Cut and Paste' series.

8 'Vertical Clock', its hands
moving vertically in a glass
cloche stacked on a green
table on a mirrored pedestal.

9 'Eat!', part of the Berengo
Glass 'Drink!Eat!Fun!Rest!
Think!Dream!Love!' series
of sculptural Murano glass
objects.

10 'Fun!' symbolizes the
enchantment of life, its
trumpet and balloon just
wide enough to hold a
beautiful flower.

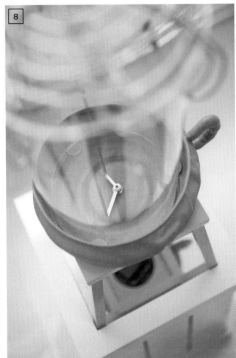

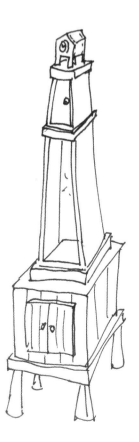

Studio mhl

NETHERLANDS

A cute porcelain button on your ring finger, a ravishing hand-stitched tree on your lapel, a delicate landscape on a ceramic plaque: these are just a few of the charming treasures to be found in Monique van Bruggen's imaginative trove. Her career is a story of well-timed collaborations and fortunate connections – her family, for a start. Her mother used to design jewelry and thereby amassed stacks of beads and buttons. Monique fell into the same artistic pot, and, after graduating from the Design Academy in Eindhoven and the jewelry faculty of the Gerrit Rietveld Academy in Amsterdam, started her own jewelry design studio, mhl. For a while she shared an atelier in the centre of Amsterdam with fellow artist Afke Golsteijn, but then she decided to work from home, producing her own collections and carrying out freelance work, all the while working part-time in a milk factory. Then a good friend introduced her to Frank Visser of IJM Studio – a pivotal encounter. 'That was an amazing experience,' recounts Monique. 'Frank has a great studio in Amsterdam, where he makes the most beautiful things. He makes his own sets for photo shoots and collaborates with photographers. I have made jewelry out of fabric and tiny cakes out of buttons as display material for a Dutch children's clothing brand, painted sets for new shoots, made big murals as backgrounds for photography, hand-made paper flowers, designed textile prints … just to name a few of the wonderful craft projects I've been involved in.' During this period, Monique met jewelry designer Bonne van der Ree, and the pair decided to share a studio in the Jordaan district of Amsterdam. 'Having my own workplace enables me to define and strengthen my own handwriting. Both the use of subtle colours and beautiful materials – mother-of-pearl buttons and delicate illustrations on porcelain – are very important to me. I like to make things as much as possible by hand and use small, found objects,' she says. Her surroundings also influence her craft. Her pieces tend to be more intimate and dainty when she works from a small atelier, whereas when she works with IJM Studio it is more expansive and generous. Each of Monique's past encounters with creative minds has led to a burst of inspiration. For that reason, we cannot wait to see what her next artistic collaboration will be.

See also p. 279
www.studio-mhl.com

1 Pouring liquid clay on a plaster plate to form random-sized brooches. Once rounded and smoothed, they will be baked in the oven.

2 Illustrations by Monique van Bruggen for Frank Visser of IJM Studio. Each drawing is made by painting and cutting thin paper strips, then gluing them in place.

3 Still life: handmade brooches, button jewelry, Japanese masking tape and *Bonheur*, a book by Keiko Minami.

4 The poetry of the packaging is a good indicator of what will be found inside: each piece of jewelry is packed in a little box stamped with a drawing.

5 Pretty little things: sterling silver necklaces with handmade porcelain medallions featuring a raised drawing, silver birds and flowers, and amazonite beads.

6 Sterling silver 'Button' rings with glass, resin and mother-of-pearl buttons, all tied together with sewing thread.

7 'High Up in the Trees' brooch set of glazed porcelain with a pencil drawing.

8 Take a real branch, tie some thread around it and paint it, then tape and stitch on some paper leaves, and you too may end up with an adorable posy like this one.

Susan Dwyer

USA

Although Susan Dwyer focused on sculpture at the School of the Art Institute of Chicago, she never explored the ceramics department. When she arrived at art school, she planned to study figure painting but ended up spending four years making inflated vinyl installations and stuffed yellow bumper sculptures. At the time she had no idea how versatile and elegant ceramic materials could be. Once she had been out of college for a few years, she found herself wanting to produce sculpture that was accessible yet beautiful. An idea for a water tower structure had been stuck in her head for a while, and after a few months she decided to make it. She knew it had to be made out of clay, so she signed up at a local ceramics studio and started producing the work. Her water towers soon led to simpler constructions, in the form of further functional structures found in industry. She executed some of her designs with reinforced papier-mâché in order to create far thinner forms than would be possible with clay. 'It wasn't long before I debuted that first small collection on the web, and I've been delighted with the warm response ever since,' she says. This unexpected career development led to more refined work, but Susan still maintained her core interest in volume and the physical relationship between people and structures. As she says: 'Form never follows function more directly than it does in the urban landscape, and I love the challenge of recalling the elegance and modernity of those utilitarian forms.' She is deeply interested in exploring standard materials such as clay and paper, and giving them an unforeseen grace. The softness of the shapes and the ambiguity of materials give her work an irresistible tactility, and she is delighted when people have an emotional response to her creations. 'I'm always thrilled when someone picks up one of my pieces and experiences a moment of surprise or satisfaction,' she says. Susan is right to be thrilled, but what most people feel when holding one of her delicate, gold-embellished pieces is more than surprise and satisfaction; it is pure joy.

See also pp. 255, 296
www.upintheairsomewhere.com

1

2

1 Simply resplendent: 'Gold Paper Bowl' set, in papier-mâché, acrylic paint, polyurethane and gold leaf.

2 'Tall Paper Bowls' in progress, like two hybrid eggs from a mythical species.

3 The golden touch: applying gold leaf.

4 Utilitarian but sculptural vessels for your dearest guests: earthenware 'Dip Cups and Pitcher' with glaze and rubber.

3

4

221

Susie Cowie
UK

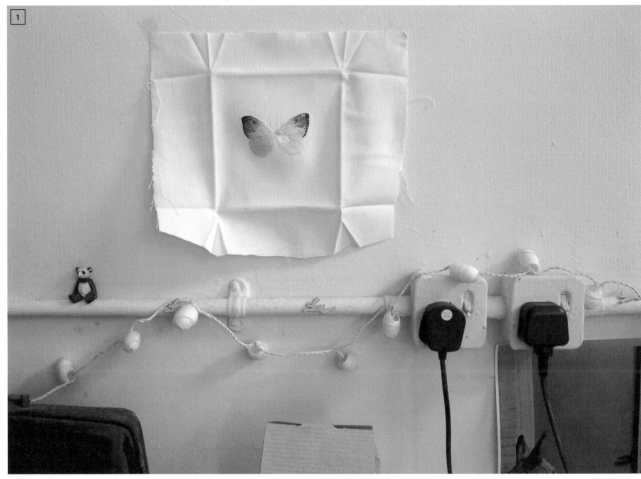

1 Miniature wonder:
  tiny Union Jack flags
  incorporated into butterfly
  wings in 'Union Jack
  Butterfly' embroidery.

2 Susie Cowie in her
  workshop, embroidering
  with nimble fingers.

3 'Dark Lace', lace panel over
  appliqué silk.

Susie Cowie lives in the heart of an historic and artistic neighbourhood in East London. She is passionate about art (particularly paintings by Gustav Klimt and Cy Twombly), cycling around London, learning about Oriental cultures, the Victoria and Albert Museum, and old French textiles. In relaxed moments she professes to enjoy photographing cakes and drinking tea in London's beautiful cafes. When she is working, she is a freelance embroidery designer with an exceptional flair for beauty. She applies her precise technique and her fine sense for poetry to turning vintage and non-vintage fabrics into various creations, the most spectacular of which look like lace. Since graduating from Glasgow School of Art with honours in textile design, Susie has gained growing recognition for her sensitive and innovative work. Her artistic skills combine not only a remarkable dexterity in embroidery but also an intuitive ability to link creative design, graphic illustration and commercial practicality. Some of her earliest work was purchased by US lifestyle store Anthropologie and by British retailer Marks &

Spencer for bedlinen. Susie has also collaborated with fashion designer Margaret Howell on a limited collection of underwear items. Her client list is impressive, and includes Calvin Klein Homeware, Victoria's Secret, J. Crew, Banana Republic and Gap. Other projects have seen her produce exquisite costume embroidery for films. For *Young Victoria* she supplied some four metres of fabric for just one period dress, and for *Bright Star*, about the life of the poet John Keats, she developed the design for and hand-embroidered a pillow slip that Keats is given, which turns out to be central to a pivotal moment in the story. Susie's other projects have included illustrative embroidery for magazines and exhibitions, and she has also led embroidery workshops, one entitled 'Creative Embroidery: Learning to Observe'. Susie's work certainly has the power to put us in a contemplative, almost meditative state. Her gentle delicacy could melt any hard heart.

See also pp. 250, 280
www.susiecowie.com

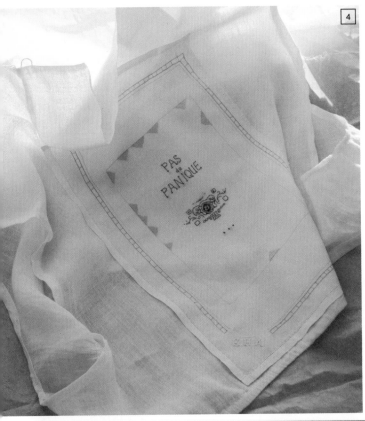

4 'Pas de Panique', a vintage handkerchief embroidered by Susie and applied to a vintage blouse.

5 A personal photograph, a postcard and the body of a decapitated Swarovski panda, among other intimate ephemera.

6 How to beautify the mundane: two embroidery designs applied onto simple waiter's notebooks.

7 Exquisite floral embroidery on silk organdie in 'Anemone White'.

8 The 'Pansy Colour Study' gathers flower appliqués in rope embroidery onto a vintage ballet-pink silk handkerchief.

9 'Pansy Colour Study' and 'Anemone White' are layered together for a poetic moment.

SuTurno

SPAIN

A strong use of geometric shapes, a twist brought by hand, and a commitment to using traditional materials that will eventually attain a more contemporary look: this is the signature recipe for most projects by SuTurno, the Spanish design studio based in Madrid. Founders Julia Vergara and Javier Gutierrez can often be found browsing in second-hand shops and flea markets, or travelling the world to discover new craft traditions. Collecting objects is one of their passions and their main source of inspiration: pottery, records, wooden objects and scraps of fabric accumulate in their studio, a live-in inspiration box. The duo design strong prints and patterns (on commission for fashion clients), generally using manual techniques. Their recent ventures range from clay tiles and cushions to tote bags and scarves. The charming format of the little tiles is in line with Julia's geometric artworks and organic shapes. Their rough, 'not-so-perfect' texture is preserved with a matt finish, intensifying the handmade feel of each tile. SuTurno's original patterns were created with the help of handmade rubber stamps, commonly used in many of their designs. The different colours are applied by hand before the tiles are taken to the oven. The result is a unique product that combines traditional functional elements with a contemporary look. The inspiration behind SuTurno's cushions, meanwhile, can be found in traditional Spanish textiles, especially the so-called *espiga* style. This distinctive herringbone pattern is first hand-drawn, then silkscreened onto cotton fabric for the front of each cushion, but the original *espiga* fabric is used on the back – once again, a fine harmony between the present and the past. All of SuTurno's products are made locally in strictly limited runs, and their vision is to counteract mass production, mass consumption and seasonal trends. Whenever they undertake a new project, they aim to create designs that are timeless and authentic. Witnessing the natural ageing effect on a product, respecting the beauty of an imperfection, these are paramount to SuTurno's embrace of conscientious artisanship.

See also pp. 301, 307, 315
www.suturno.net

1

2

226

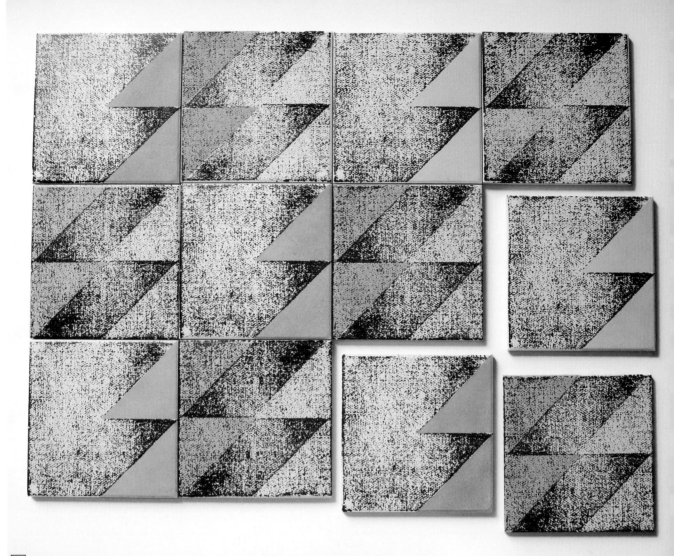

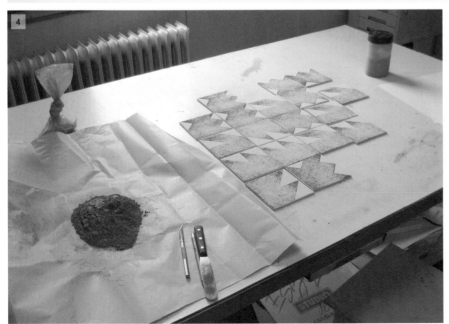

4

1 SuTurno's reinterpretation of the traditional *espiga* pattern: a finished cushion is displayed against its herringbone silkscreen.

2 The herringbone pattern is first hand-drawn, an extremely fine and precise exercise.

3 Each clay tile is silkscreened by hand, using vitrifiable pigments, before being baked.

4 Silkscreened tiles, ready to be sent to the oven, next to a sheet holding leftover pigment powder used to create the paint for the silkscreen printing.

Suzie Stanford

AUSTRALIA

2

The essence of Suzie Stanford's ethos can be summed up in one wonderful word: 'upcycling'. 'By employing old materials in new products,' she says, 'I find it inspiring to be able to incorporate the unique histories of each item I use. I put things together that are not supposed to be together and hope that by my works' celebration of colour and by juxtaposing the old with the new, my pieces make people smile.' From an early age Suzie made things, but the sudden death of her inspirational father made her face up to the fact that we are not going to be around forever, so she decided to make the most of her creativity and launched her own design practice. Every one of her products is handmade in her sun-drenched Melbourne studio, a haven for her excesses, resonating with optimism for the potential usefulness of everything and overflowing with collections of items waiting for just the right project. On finding a hoard of old tea towels, Suzie was inspired to create furniture upholstery. From this collection she moved onto using found tapestries, which are her favourite pieces, a celebration of true handcraft. Each tapestry in the patchwork upholstery took hundreds of hours to complete, as it had to be fitted to size, a real labour of love. 'With so many mass-produced products around us, my work is a break away from a certain sameness that flattens out individual expression,' notes Suzie. Ideas for pieces come to her quickly, though seeing her concepts through can lead her on unexpected journeys. 'One week I'll be working closely with steel fabricators to make a base for a champagne-cork chandelier. The next, I'll spend forever searching every auction house in town for a particular furniture shape for a one-off upholstered piece, or I'll make long road trips hunting for second-hand pieces to anchor a client's fit-out theme. Colour informs most of my creative decisions,' she explains. Her work is sold through trendsetting stores such as Liberty in London and Lane Crawford in the Far East. She also receives commissions from clients wishing to bring a piece of their family background into the living room. 'I think this warm response comes as the pieces strike a chord with their own journey,' she muses, 'and they touch a powerful vein of nostalgia and ironic wit, while providing a place of comfort that envelops memories.'

See also pp. 266, 292
www.suziestanford.com

1 'Crown Jewels by Suzie Stanford': a workshop like a modern-day Ali Baba's cave, overflowing with jewelry made from insects set in resin, bangles of marching creatures, and sterling silver necklaces adorned with bugs, silver charms and rock crystals.

2 Mona Lisa tapestries surface amid a productive chaos: all the master upholsterer's tools and devices are within reach.

3

4

5

6

imagination . . .
will take you everywhere

3 & 4 Bespoke door handles, made from found brass treasures, in the 'Handshake' collection: on one side a peacock perches on a swan, on the other little creatures hitch a ride on a dolphin.

5 & 6 The exuberant 'Holiday' collection, made with upcycled 1960s/70s beach towels, is a bright and beautiful proposition.

Vera João Espinha

PORTUGAL

Perdi o fio à meada is a colloquial Portuguese expression, meaning someone has 'lost the thread [of a conversation]'. Vera João Espinha turned this into 'I lost the wool thread', a particularly apt name for her handcrafted accessory brand. Most of her creations are made using crochet, the core and signature technique that delights her growing customer base. As a child, she learned to crochet with her grandmother. 'When I became more familiar with the crochet hooks,' she recalls, 'I started making clothes for my dolls. Since I can remember, I have always liked to crochet or knit, and my favourite pieces were blankets.' Vera studied graphic design at the Antonio Arroio School of Arts in Lisbon, and attended drawing and painting classes at the city's National Society of Fine Arts. She works as a graphic designer for a book publisher, while dedicating her spare time to her ambitious craft project, which has already earned her an honourable mention at a contemporary jewelry competition in Portugal. 'An accessory to be worn should be comfortable,' she states. 'We need to feel that a bracelet or a necklace is part of our body.' Vera's main sources of inspiration are the natural artifacts she collects. Stones, leaves, branches and seeds are organic flotsam and jetsam

that fascinate her, along with the colours in a certain photograph, a particular painting, her grandmother's doilies or recycled objects she has created with her daughter. 'The part I like most in my work is creating the first piece,' she says. 'This "laboratory" process is important. I need time to try things out and to receive feedback from friends and family.' The needle becomes her pencil. She does not sketch and lets the ideas appear spontaneously. Most collections can only be reproduced in small series, as they are all handmade and take considerable time to be completed. 'When creating a new work, inevitably I start to think about the next one. I follow my taste and feelings rather than fashion trends, looking for timeless pieces rather than going with the flow. Combining unlikely colours, discovering new visual harmonies and shapes is the way I experiment,' she says. Vera likes to spend time finetuning compositions that include natural elements within the crochet. She thus creates a compelling fusion of traditional techniques, contemporary designs and unassuming organic treasures. The wool thread is never lost.

See also pp. 273, 309, 311
http://perdi-o-fio-a-meada.blogspot.com

1 Cheery stripes will keep you warm: wool leftovers from projects are often used to create hot water bottles and pot holders.

2 Vera João Espinha hand-knitting an 'Ábaco' jewelry piece with woollen thread.

3 A handful, or two, of delicious crochet woollen beads.

4 Craft it, style it, wear it: the 'Bambu' necklace made with mercerized cotton and glass beads.

5 Drawing from both the past and present, Vera takes inspiration from technical books and her grandmother's crocheted mats.

7

6

8

9

6 People may not look you in the eye when you're wearing the 'Flor de Inverno' brooch of cotton thread and pompons.

7 Joyful yet elegant garland neckpiece, or 'Colar Fio de Ovos', of mercerized cotton and steel wire.

8 One for every day of the week: 'Meia Casca' brooches, made with cotton thread and a metal pin.

9 'Pinha' pins: real pinecones, embedded in adorable mercerized cotton cupules.

10 Vera folds boxes to prepare a delivery, while modelling her 'Colar Fio de Ovos' necklace.

11 Keep it close to your chest: the 'Bolsa' necklace, made with cotton thread, holds a little stone inside, waiting to be replaced with your own cherished token.

11

Wauw Design

DENMARK

1 Welcome and please take a seat: the porcelain elements of the 'Songlines', 'Raw', 'Basalt' and 'Lamp' collections are highly complementary.

2 Milk or sugar? The plump porcelain teapot, sugar bowl and cream pot from the 'Songlines' range.

3 Any flower or branch would look divine in one of these 'Basalt' vases, whose black glazed surface holds a shimmering attraction.

Wow! We can hardly hold back our reaction on first glimpsing the beautiful simplicity of these gorgeous ceramics. Just spell the word a little differently and you get the highly appropriate company name, 'Wauw'. Its founders, Danish/Dutch design duo Sussi and Maranke, work from a studio in Copenhagen. Both received their professional training at the Danish Design School's Institute of Ceramics and Glass. One grew up in the countryside of southern Fynen, the other in the industrial port of Rotterdam. Two very different backgrounds, but two very similar sensibilities for creating contemporary and stylish tableware and home accessories. The duo make high-quality products in ceramics and also glass, always with the emphasis on great design, true craftsmanship and sustainable production. 'Our studio is a "fantasy laboratory", where our ideas come to life,' they say. 'The creative process is something between an obsession and an addiction. Not working with ceramics and with each other is simply unthinkable.' The pair like to experiment. 'We are constantly working on developing new glazes and shapes. Opening the kiln after a new test can be a joy or a disaster. The self-made glazes

we use can be quite a struggle. But the happiness that comes with opening a kiln with "wauw" results is definitely worth the trouble!' Wauw Design products are wedged and hand-thrown in porcelain clay, meaning that every item in a product range has a unique individual touch. Tableware can be found in the 'Raw' collection, characterized by a graphic decorative spiral groove running from top to bottom, and in the exquisite 'Crystal' collection, which showcases a unique technique of crystal glazing. Sussi and Maranke have also created thin semi-transparent porcelain pendant lights that come with wiring in ten different colours: a nice decorative element that – beautifully – meets people's expectations of functional yet clever objects. 'We are inspired by everyday life,' the pair say. 'Things we hear on the street, a journey, an image, the structure of a wall, the bark of a tree, the formation of ice crystals on a window, or a good find in a trash can.' We are most fortunate to be on the receiving end of the results of these lucid moments of inspiration.

See also pp. 263, 287, 303
www.wauw-design.dk

Wauw Design

4 Throwing-wheel, where the base of a porcelain cup is being trimmed.

5 The closet, where products are stored to dry before going into the kiln for their first firing.

6 Glaze tests are indispensable when it is time to try out different colours at the start of a new collection.

7 Uninterrupted clear sky ahead: these ice-blue 'Crystal' vases have a unique crystal glaze finish that emits a beautiful iridescence.

Wiebke Meurer

SWITZERLAND

1 A highly mechanical workshop, with heavy machinery and tools, in contrast to the graceful metalwork produced and hung on the wall like hard-earned trophies.

2 A sight of lightness to come: a butterfly newly cut out of a silver sheet.

3 'Metallblumen Wachsen' derives from the decorative ornaments traditionally painted on porcelain. The floral silver pattern breaks away from the porcelain cup that once contained it.

Gold flowers painted on a porcelain cup grow out of the two-dimensional surface into open air, while threads of silver creep over onto the white porcelain spaces. Floral decoration transforms into three-dimensional ornament, and what remains is a porcelain vessel adorned with fine metal lace. It is a powerful force that enables decor to free itself from object. In the 'Metallblumen Wachsen' series, porcelain and metal seem to grow out of each other. Swiss artist and silversmith Wiebke Meurer is fascinated by historical European works of silver, gold and porcelain. The combination of materials dates back to eighteenth-century Europe, when the upper classes would serve desserts on porcelain vessels next to exuberant pieces of precious metalwork. Most of Wiebke's creations seem to have come straight out of an art collection from the past, but they have been freed from their historical context and original metalwork heritage. 'I explore traditional ways to design objects, not to stick to tradition but because I use tradition as a starting point for my creative strategies,' she says. In her 'Flying High' piece, a deer wanders about nonchalantly, no longer the companion of the goddess Diana. In another work,

'The Broken Chinese', the decor has unleashed a destructive force that has turned a broken object into something new. Wiebke is not concerned about the restoration of the broken object: she wants to deconstruct it, to reach the heart of its integrity and reinvent it, both formally and functionally. In 'Service Royal', she was inspired by the porcelain service of Louis XVI – 400 pieces ordered in 1783 from Sèvres, for the king's personal use. This fabulously sumptuous service was one of the most ambitious designs ever manufactured at Sèvres; it also represented pure power, wealth and the highest aesthetics of the time. The dishes were regarded as an extension of the king's body and their decoration as an act of royal worship. Wiebke's 'Service Royal' is just as beautiful in appearance as the original, but only the decorative elements remain. Her service has no meaning other than as a representation of its own beauty. Through her innovative and sophisticated fusion of metal and porcelain, Wiebke is able to experiment with tableware and cutlery like a masterful alchemist, always seeking new and extraordinary combinations.

See also p. 292
www.wiebkemeurer.com

2 3

4 & 5 The 'Service Royal', a copper-gold-plate and porcelain masterwork, inspired by court intrigues and historical expenses on sumptuous, superfluous, luxury items.

6

7

6 & 7 The 'Talking Pieces'
series is a contemporary
take on historical silverware.
Mundane objects are
decorated with details
and coated with a layer of
precious metal, each piece
portraying a miniature
world that conveys both
tenderness and wealth.

Xenia Taler

CANADA

Welcome to a busy Ontario tile studio, where works that are beautifully executed and a pure joy to look at are gold standards. Xenia Taler explains how she got started: 'My partner Steven Koblinsky's mother suggested I might earn money by painting custom backsplashes and she introduced me to another tile artist, who explained to me about china paint and over-glaze enamels.' Within a couple of months, Xenia had put her first pieces up for sale at craft shows. Once the production became too demanding for her alone, Steven stepped in and many things changed. 'I saw the tiles as little paintings, and wasn't concerned about how I obtained my glazes,' says Xenia. 'Steven had a different attitude and a more refined sensitivity to materials. He identified that we were working in a craft medium. If we were ever to gain any recognition, we would have to master both materials and processes.' Steven invested in a set of digital scales, studied ceramics books, bought raw ingredients and learned about clay and glazes. The couple moved to a 'real' studio and started participating in trade shows, where they sold directly to stores. 'This was the late 1990s, which was a good time for craft in North America. We were able to grow our business in those first few years while developing a loyal customer base,' Xenia explains. 'Today there's more competition from low-priced, mass-produced goods. "Design" has replaced "Craft", which is more about knowledge and quality.' Xenia and Steven advocate and celebrate a subtle and restrained approach, one closer to a mid-century understanding of craft. Their studio is focused on decoration and hand-painting. The images, and the way in which they are created, are principally what set the collections apart and attract people's interest. Although theirs is a small studio, with limited facilities, they maintain attention by continually introducing as many new designs as a larger company would. Hand-painting allows small runs of a wide range of designs without loss of productivity. 'My design focus consists of creating images that are simple enough to hand-paint repeatedly, but not so simple that they become generic,' says Xenia. She often looks to folk art for inspiration and says she is 'always rewarded with some new way to use dots, lines and simple geometric elements in new combinations and varieties'. How delightful for us that this is the case.

See also p. 258
www.xeniataler.com

1 The busy ceramic workshop
   packed with equipment,
   storage and works-in-
   progress.

2 Like a curator pulling out
   a shelf of rare illustrations,
   Steven Koblinsky displays
   exquisite tile trials.

3 Xenia Taler must have
   left in a hurry; she left
   her glasses behind on the
   painting desk, where her
   whimsical drawings get their
   spectacular colour.

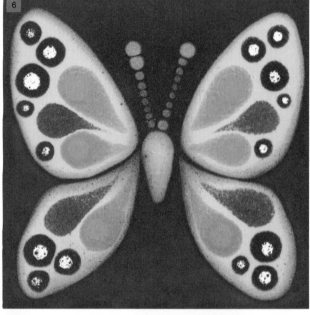

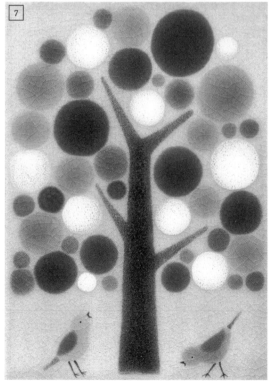

4 Sweetness, a touch of naïvety and some folk resonance epitomize Xenia's painting style in her ceramic tile collection, as in this charming 'First Snow' scene.

5 'Owl' ceramic tile in ochre.

6 'Monarch Butterfly' on brown ceramic tile.

7 'Canopy' ceramic tile.

8 The main activity of the workshop is producing collectible tiles, but it also offers contemporary homewares, such as these 'Crayon' vases.

9 Functional yet highly decorative, these 'Kimono' trivets would also look good on a wall.

Art

ATSUKO ISHII

1 Come Out and Play
Large etching, numbered and signed.

2 Hirondelle No. 5
Artist book, illustrated with exclusive etchings.

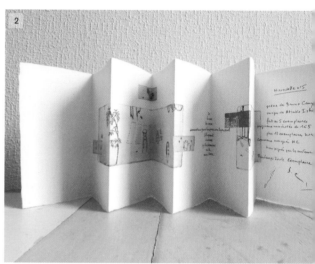

ANNA EMILIA LAITINEN

3 Snow House
Painting.

4 Untitled painting
Painting for the cover of *Vieläkö kukkivat omenapuut?* (Are the apple trees still blooming?), a book by Helena Miettinen.

DEPEAPA

5 Niña gorro
Pen drawing.

6 Pareja tetera
Pen and ink drawing.

ROHAN EASON

7 White Rabbit, White Rabbit, White Rabbit
Illustration, 'Without Alice' series.

8 The Piano in the Forest
Illustration for *Anna & the Witch's Bottle*, a children's book by Geoff Cox, published by Black Maps Press.

SUSIE COWIE

1 Name Lace
Prototype lace sample of
a christening gift.

2 The Barber of Seville
Lace design intended for a project
with the Royal Opera House, Covent
Garden, London.

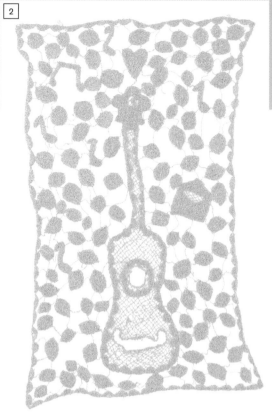

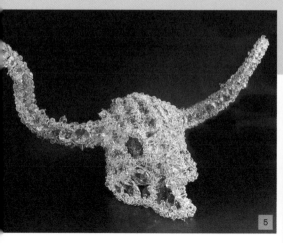

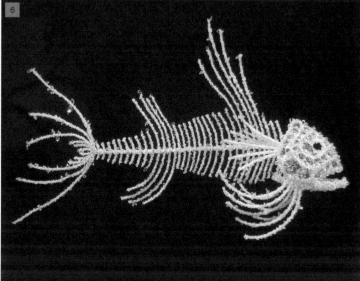

AURÉLIE WILLIAM LEVAUX

3 Cauchemar
Ink and embroidery on cotton, from the book *Les Yeux du Seigneur.*

4 11
Ink and embroidery on cotton, from the book *Les Yeux du Seigneur.*

GÉRALDINE GONZALEZ

5 Cow
Crystal sculpture.

6 Fish
Crystal sculpture.

7 Coral
Crystal sculpture.

8 The Table
Papier-mâché still-life installation.

JANIS HEEZEN

1 Burn
Hand-stitching and acrylic paint on cotton.

2 Violence
Hand-stitching and acrylic paint on cotton.

3 Untitled: exotic bird
Hand-stitching and acrylic paint on cotton.

4 Power
Hand-stitching and acrylic paint on cotton.

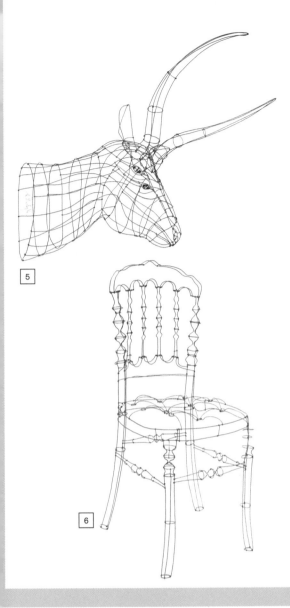

MARIE CHRISTOPHE

5 Himpala
Wire sculpture.

6 Catillon Chair
Wire sculpture for fashion and
lifestyle luxury house, Roger Vivier.

7 Lampe Eléphant
Wire sculpture and lamp.

SEVERIJA INČIRAUSKAITĖ-KRIAUNEVIČIENĖ

8 & 9 Sculptures
Old rusty metal wares, drilling and
cotton cross-stitching, 'Autumn
Collection' series.

Ceramics

STUDIO KIKI VAN EIJK

1 Stamped and Sealed vase
Glazed porcelain.

2 Soft candle-holder
White porcelain.

ALEXA LIXFELD

3 Concrete tableware
Concrete with wajima nuri lacquerware finish, 'Collector' collection.

4 Kubus vessels
Solid coloured porcelain: outside matt, inside glazed.

5 Circle bowl
Concrete, in white.

1

2

3

5

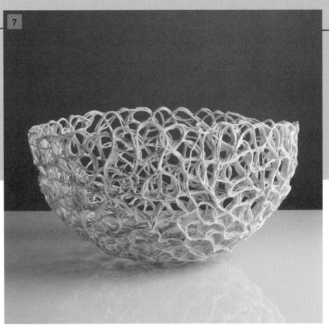

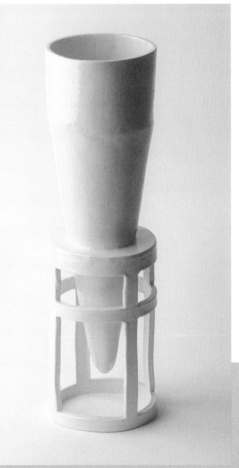

SILKE DECKER

6 Cordporcelain candle-holders
White porcelain with gold rim.

7 Cordporcelain bowl
Coral-patterned white porcelain.

SUSAN DWYER

**8 Building A, B and C
vases/containers**
Earthenware and glaze, 'Factory
Vessel' series.

9 Vase/container
Earthenware and glaze 'Water
Tower' series.

CYNTHIA VARDHAN

1 Large Vase
Porcelain and pigmented slips, 'Functional Art' collection.

2 Teacup Pair
Porcelain and pigmented slips, 'Functional Art' collection.

3 Three Pieces, Three Views sculptures
Stoneware and slips, 'Weather is here, wish you were nice' series.

BAILEY DOESN'T BARK

4 Dots does
23-carat gold dots design on natural white porcelain, 'Dots' collection.

5 Candles and plates
'Jae' soy candles on handmade natural white porcelain plates from the 'Dots', 'Ants on my Plate' and 'Four Seasons' series.

ATELIER POLYHEDRE

6 Fémur vase
Matt white glazed faience.

7 Oeil pour œil Bombe
White glazed faience with gold.

8 Vanité money-box
Glazed faience with gold.

6

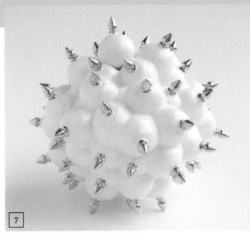

7

9

8

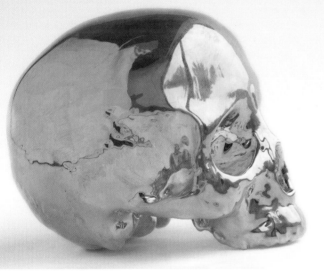

10

11

MEL ROBSON

By Hand bowls
ress-moulded porcelain and
toneware with decals.

**0 The Absence of Objects
detail)**
lipcast porcelain with decals.

**1 Keep Calm and Carry On
Pigeon)**
lipcast porcelain.

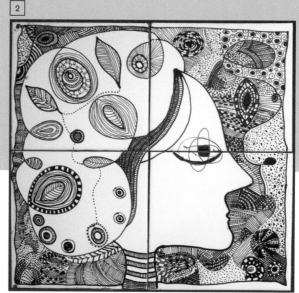

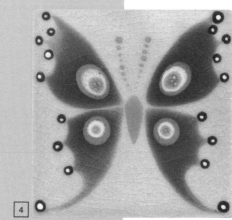

PAULA JUCHEM

1 Favela tilework
Painted mural.

2 Face tilework
Painted mural.

XENIA TALER

3 Fancy Chick – Fredda tile
Ceramic.

4 Starlight Butterfly on Grey tile
Ceramic.

5 Criss Cross vase
Ceramic.

6 Fish School trivets
Ceramic.

7 Festive Flowers tile
Ceramic.

258

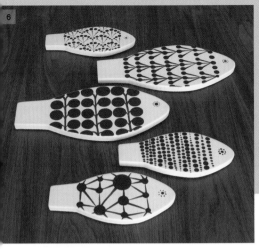

NORA ROCHEL

8, 9, 10 & 11 Vases
Coloured porcelain, glazed on the
inside.

1

3

2

4

NATHALIE CHOUX

1 Les Radis salt and pepper set
Porcelain.

2 Coloquinte vase
Porcelain, with little character as lid.

3 Assiette au doriphore plate
Porcelain.

4 Vase
Porcelain, with handle.

LAURA STRASSER

**5 With Love From China
self-portrait sculpture**
Porcelain.

ANGUS & CELESTE

6 Clap Clap Mr Giraffe wall tile
Glazed porcelain.

7 Pomegranate Large vase
Glazed porcelain.

8 True Blue Large vase
Glazed porcelain.

9 Gum Nut Bottle vase
Glazed porcelain.

10 Star Blossom Bottle vase
Glazed porcelain.

SISSEL WATHNE

1 Knitted Cylinders
High-fired porcelain.

2 A Picture tableware series (detail)
High-fired porcelain, with transparent glaze and traditional gold decoration.

LARS RANK

3 Sta'vasen candle-holders/vases
Porcelain, in green.

4 Sta'vasen candle-holders/vases
Porcelain, in white.

5 Weeds – Clover candle-holders
Parian porcelain.

6 The Tilted Lighthouse tealight-holders
Parian porcelain.

WAUW DESIGN

7 Vases (small, medium and large)
Porcelain, 'Crystal Spring 2010' collection.

8 Ice Blue vases
Porcelain, 'Crystal Spring 2010' collection.

9 Lyshuse candle-holders/vases
Porcelain, 'Raw' collection.

10 Vases (small, medium and large)
Porcelain, in soft pink, red and white, 'Crystal Spring 2010' collection.

Ceramics

1

2

6

3

5

4

ATELIER POLYHEDRE

1 Siphon plate
Black glazed faience.

2 Extend Beurrier butter dish and saucer
Black glazed faience.

3 Skin Tasse cup
Black glazed faience.

SARAH CIHAT

4 Black Wolf sculpture
Porcelain, 'Dirt' collection.

5 Black Dogwood vases
Dipped in white porcelain, 'Dirt' collection.

6 FvsS candle and diffuser
Joya fragrance, in black.

SOPHIE COOK

7 Cowboy pod vase
Black-design porcelain.

8 Vases
Porcelain; various shapes – pod, bottle, teardrop; various colours – matt light grey, grey, clear, graphite.

IKUKO IWAMOTO

9 Spikyspiky vases
Porcelain, set of two, in white.

10 Spikyspiky bowls
Porcelain, set of two, in black and white.

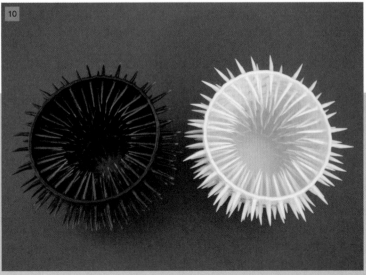

Furniture

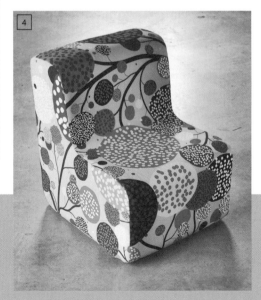

SUZIE STANFORD

1 & 2 Armchairs
Re-upholstered with embroidery canvases, 'Tapestry Furniture' collection.

ATELIER R. BERNIER

3 Floor stool
Round, 'Zig, Boom!' fabric collection.

4 Easy chair
Low armless, 'Fleurs pompon rós' fabric collection.

5 Floor stool
Square, 'Fleurs pompon rós' fabric collection.

6 Coffee table
Pyrographed wood.

JEAN PELLE

7 Vanity cabinet
Cabinet, with face lamp and extendable mirror, 'Assemblage' series.

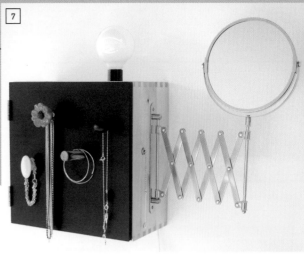

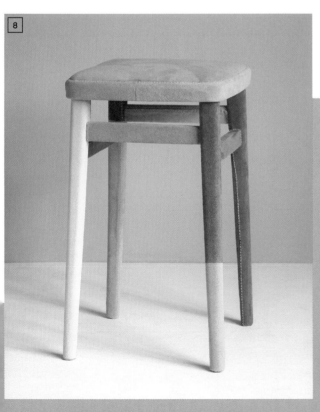

SOOJIN KANG

8 Stool
Partly re-upholstered with suede,
'Dressed Furniture' series.

9 Dining chair
Partly re-upholstered with suede,
'Dressed Furniture' series.

JEN DESCHÊNES

1 Chair No. 2 of 6
Hand-screenprinted vintage French
linen, *c.* 1920–30, on Georgian
mahogany balloon-back chair.

JAMESPLUMB

2 For Richer For Poorer chair
Antique chair with cast concrete,
'Concrete Stitches' series.

3 To Have and To Hold chair
Antique duo chair with cast concrete,
'Concrete Stitches' series.

4 For Better For Worse chair
Antique chair with cast concrete,
'Concrete Stitches' series.

STUDIO KIKI VAN EIJK

5 At Home seat and cabinet
Tulip wood and ceramic, 'Zuiderzee Settings' series.

6 Homecrafts cabinet with integrated fold-back ironing board
Tulip wood and ceramic, 'Zuiderzee Settings' series.

7 Room Divider (back view)
Lurex, viscose, cotton and nickel-plated steel, 'Domestic Jewels' series.

8 Catching Fish trolley
Tulip wood and ceramic, 'Zuiderzee Settings' series.

Glass

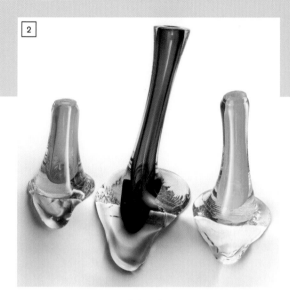

ESQUE STUDIO

1 Hot Pop vase
Pink glass under fuchsia, with varied coloured discs.

2 Drippy vases
Large and small, in cherry, smoke and orange glass.

3 Doy Lee bowl
White and fuchsia glass.

4 Dribble vases
Large and small, in amber, light ruby and fuchsia glass.

5

6

7

SIA MAI

5 Containers
Glass with yellow elastic, set of two, 'Clear Picnic' series.

6 Bottles
Clear glass, 'Bottle with Lid' series.

7 Decanter and drinking glasses
Clear glass, 'Structure' series.

8 Containers
Glass in Colour No. 8, 'Opaque Colour Picnic' series.

STUDIO KIKI VAN EIJK

9 Rest! sculpture
Glass, 'Drink!Eat!Fun!Rest!Think!Dream!Love!' series.

10 Birds Nest vase
Glass with silver decoration, 'Knick Knack Vase' series.

8

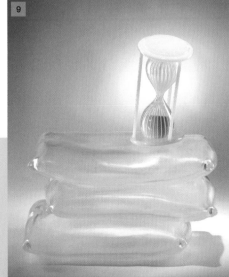

9

10

271

Jewelry

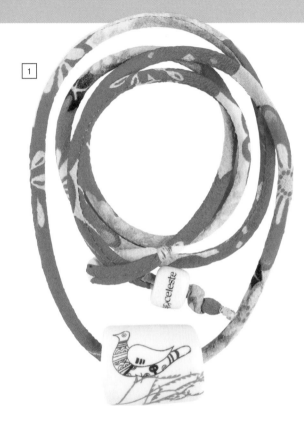

ANGUS & CELESTE

1 Perched Bird neckpiece
Kimono fabric and porcelain, 'Fabric Wraps' collection.

2 Grey and Red Blooms Winter Scarf
Pure wool and cotton print, with porcelain button.

3 Bracelets
High-fired glazed porcelain.

4 Gold Lustre Tea Cups hoop earrings
Porcelain and sterling silver.

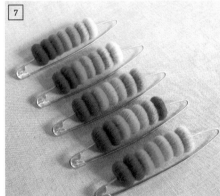

VERA JOÃO ESPINHA

5 Meia Casca brooch
Half-shell cotton crochet.

6 Ramagem brooches
Mercerized cotton crochet.

7 Alfinete Ábaco pin brooches
Wool.

8 Pulseira Fio de Ovos beaded bracelets
Mercerized cotton crochet.

9 Pulseira Ábaco bracelets
Wool.

Jewelry

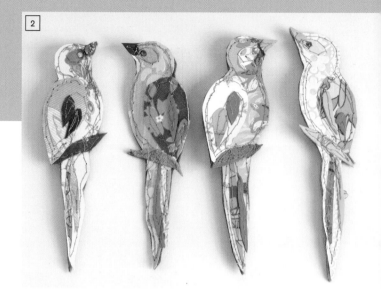

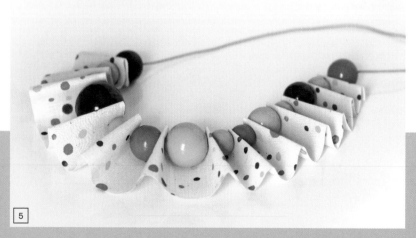

CLAIRE COLES

1 Love Story brooch
Vintage papers.

2 Bird brooches
Vintage wallpaper, leather and felt.

KRISTINA KLARIN

3 Oversized necklace
Hand-painted wooden beads in true red, misty rose, aubergine, dark peach and light beige.

4 Red, blue and white necklace
Hand-painted wooden beads and printed cotton.

5 Green, blue and aubergine necklace
Hand-painted wooden beads and printed cotton.

DEPEAPA

Gallo en la huevera brooch
Cotton, with rooster illustration.

Porcelain brooches
Varnished Russian porcelain,
with illustrations.

**Collares madera pendant
necklaces**
Wood, with illustrations.

FRIC DE MENTOL

9 & 10 Brooches
Clay, 'Flat Face' collection.

1

2

4

NORA ROCHEL

1 Ring
Whitened 925 sterling silver, ruby and zirconia.

2 Brooch
925 sterling silver and coloured porcelain.

BLANKA ŠPERKOVÁ

3 Necklace
Floral finger-knitted wire.

4 Necklace and earrings set
Finger-knitted wire.

5 Necklace and earrings set
Finger-knitted wire.

3

5

LYNDIE DOURTHE

6 Plante Grimpante pin brooches
Handmade cotton and paper.

7 Fleur 3-D brooches
Handmade cotton organdie and paper.

8 Poissons – Vanité brooches
Printed and beaded cotton.

ANTONIA ROSSI

9 & 10 Rosaries
Hand-crocheted necklaces, with fabric remnants.

Jewelry

ANNICK KRASNOPOLSKI – LES RECYCLÉS

1 Arizona neckpiece
Recycled buttons and feathers.

2 L'Aigle Noir neckpiece
Recycled tyre rubber and cowrie shells.

MELANIE BILENKER

3 Tea brooch
Gold, ebony, resin, pigment and hair.

4 One Egg brooch
Gold, ebony, resin, pigment and hair.

SOOJIN KANG

5 Watch
Antique metal watch and wool knitting, 'Wearable' collection.

6 Neckpiece
Antique metal chain and wool knitting, 'Wearable' collection.

7 Bracelet
Antique chain and resin, 'Wearable' collection.

7

6

8

9

10

11

STUDIO MHL

8 Medallion necklaces
Handmade porcelain with raised
drawing, sterling silver, beads and
stones.

9 Bracelets
Cotton or silk thread braiding, with
sterling silver details.

10 Ring
Tiny pearled-wire sterling silver ring,
with antique glass acorn, faceted
glass and silver beads.

11 Brooches
Handmade illustrated porcelain on
boxes.

Jewelry

SUSIE COWIE

1 Lace cuff
Bracelet with deer and vintage linen-covered buttons.

ANNE HOLMAN

2 Necklace
Antique pressed glass cabochon, with sterling silver setting and chain.

3 Arctic pendant
Antique map in oversized silver setting.

4 Antique Map cufflinks
Sterling silver.

5 Necklaces
'Berries' silver necklaces, roll-printed from hand-drawn etched brass plates, and 'Damask' pendant, antique black glass cabochon and silver setting.

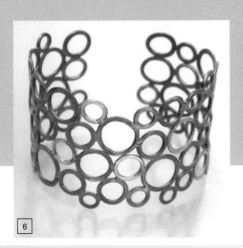

KRISTIN LORA

6 Bracelet
Oxidized sterling silver and 18-carat gold, 'Circle Cluster' collection.

7 Necklace
Sterling silver, 'Circle Link' collection.

HANNA AF EKSTRÖM

8 Parrot and Beetle necklace
Black burned steel.

9 Coral necklace
Coral and textile.

10 Crystal bracelet
Textile and quartz.

11 Knot Mask bracelet
Black burned steel and textile.

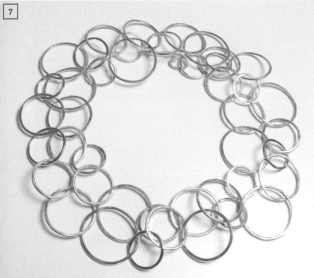

1

2

3

5

EILEEN GATT

1 Fox Amulet bangle
Oxidized silver and 18-carat gold,
with vintage button.

2 Hare and Button cufflinks
Oxidized silver.

3 Amulet Charm bracelet
Oxidized silver and 18-carat gold,
with assorted stones.

ANNA ATTERLING

4 Necklace
Oxidized silver.

5 Crown ring
925 sterling silver.

6 Angel No. 2 necklace
925 sterling silver.

KRISTIN LORA

7 Fan Brush earrings
Oxidized silver and 18-carat gold.

8 Felt Ball Grid Pin brooch
Sterling silver, with handmade felt balls.

9 Insulator necklace
Oxidized sterling silver, with recycled ceramic insulators.

10 Car earrings
Handmade oxidized sterling silver, with train-set figures and cubic zirconia.

Lighting

N°3
"TROPHÉES DE CHASSE"
collection textile

CATHRINE KULLBERG

1 Norwegian Forest
small pendant light
Birch.

ATELIER R. BERNIER

2 Datcha03 pendant shade
Oval, print on paper, 'Datcha' collection.

3 Troph 12 light
White stag printed on French Toile de Jouy fabric, 'Trophée de Chasse' collection.

JEAN PELLE

4 & 5 Button-Up lamp
Heat-resistant soft canvas shade: buttoned or unbuttoned for filtered or unfiltered light.

LAURA STRASSER

6 Vom Ribbeck pendant lights
Porcelain, pear-shaped.

7 14% pendant lights
Porcelain.

GÉRALDINE GONZALEZ

8 Méduses pendant lights
Handmade, jellyfish-shaped, paper.

9 Crâne light
Handmade, skull-shaped, paper.

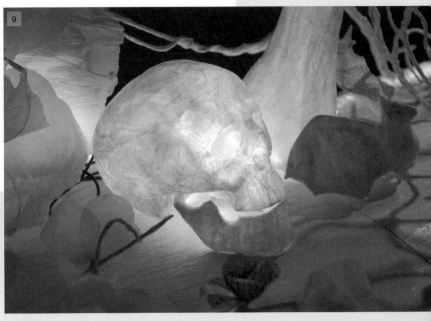

LAURA STRASSER

8 Quadrature chandelier
Set of four handmade pendant lights.

ELISA STROZYK

9 & 10 Miss Maple (on and off) pendant light
Maple wood, textile and steel, 'Wooden Textiles' collection.

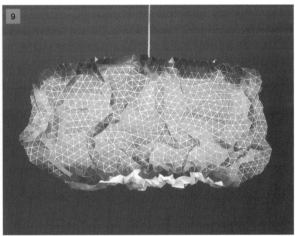

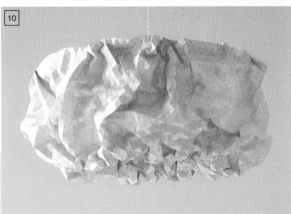

ESQUE STUDIO

1 Root Light lamp
Gold-brown glass.

AMESPLUMB

2 Cluster chandelier
Fourteen lampshades of all shapes and sizes clustered together.

STUDIO KIKI VAN EIJK

3 Dressup! lamp
Standard or pendant, with choice of three different shades.

4 Bottled lamp
Medieval-inspired glass.

WAUW DESIGN

5 Pendant lights
Thin semi-transparent porcelain, with choice of ten different coloured wires.

LARS RANK

6 Ukrudt #2 – Dandelion pendant light
Porcelain.

7 Ukrudt #1 – Gypsy Weed pendant light
Porcelain.

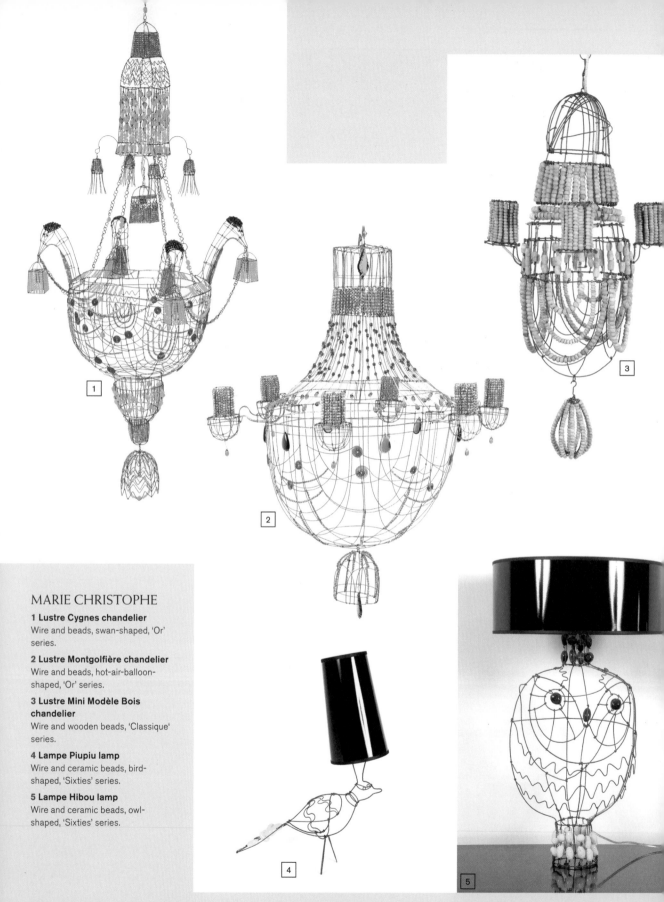

MARIE CHRISTOPHE

1 Lustre Cygnes chandelier
Wire and beads, swan-shaped, 'Or' series.

2 Lustre Montgolfière chandelier
Wire and beads, hot-air-balloon-shaped, 'Or' series.

3 Lustre Mini Modèle Bois chandelier
Wire and wooden beads, 'Classique' series.

4 Lampe Piupiu lamp
Wire and ceramic beads, bird-shaped, 'Sixties' series.

5 Lampe Hibou lamp
Wire and ceramic beads, owl-shaped, 'Sixties' series.

ROTHSCHILD & BICKERS

6 Black Nouveau pendant shades
Hand-blown black glass.

7 Spindle Pendant shade
Hand-blown borosilicate clear glass.

8 Tassel Light pendant shade
Hand-blown ruby glass.

9 Vintage Light pendant shade
Hand-blown grey glass.

10 Lantern Light pendant shade
Hand-blown bronze glass.

Metalwork

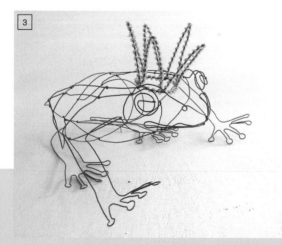

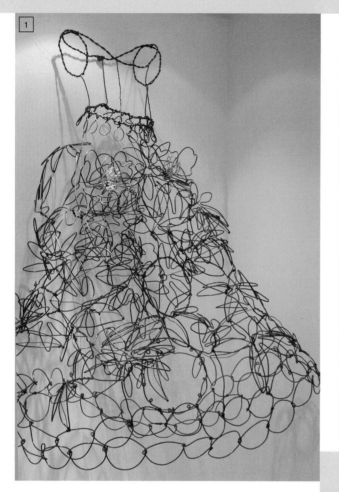

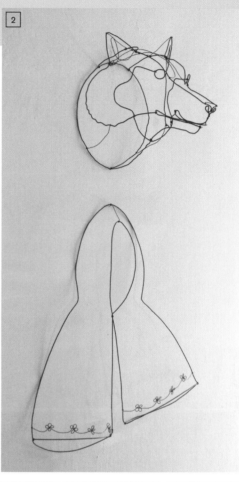

CHIZU KOBAYASHI

1 Spring Dress
Wire sculpture.

2 Little Red Riding Hood
Wire sculpture.

3 Frog Prince
Wire sculpture, with beads.

MARIA JAUHIAINEN

4 Hearts
Metal composition.

5 Lehti
Leaf-shaped silver bowl/plate.

BLANKA ŠPERKOVÁ

6 Alien
Stainless steel wire sculpture.

7 Mona Lisa
Stainless steel wire sculpture.

8 Fly Through the Head
Zinc wire sculpture.

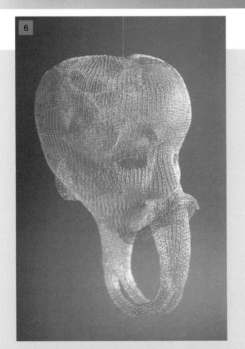

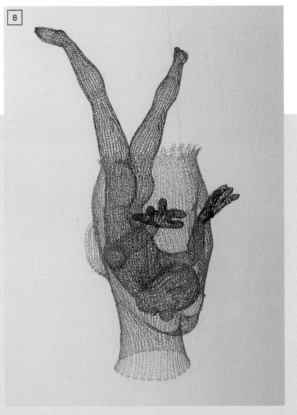

WIEBKE MEURER

1 Bambi
Silver pitcher, 'Talking Pieces' series.

2 Cup, saucer and spoon
Fine silver and porcelain,
'Metallblumen Wachsen' series.

SUZIE STANFORD

3 Clothing rack
Bespoke brass rack made for
Megan Park flagship store,
Armadale, Melbourne.

ANNA ATTERLING

4 Bowl
Oxidized 925 sterling silver.

5 Bowl
White 925 sterling silver.

6 Bowl
White 925 sterling silver.

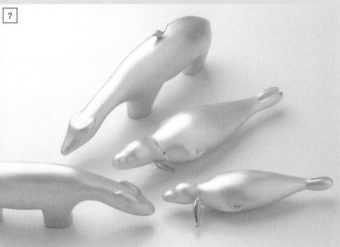

EILEEN GATT

7 Seal and Polar Bear
18-carat gold and silver sculptures.

8 Lucky Rowan
18-carat gold and silver beaker and spoon set.

9 Fox, Animal Form, Polar Bear and Hare
18-carat gold and silver beakers.

Paper and Woodwork

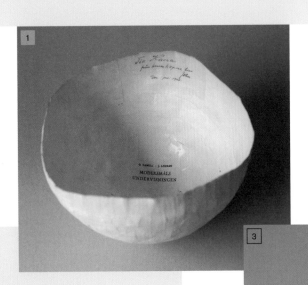

CECILIA LEVY

1 Hanna's bowl
Papier-mâché.

2 Petal bowl
Papier-mâché.

3 Neptune's Daughter's bowl
Paper.

4 & 5 The Way Out book sculpture
Illustration and needlework.

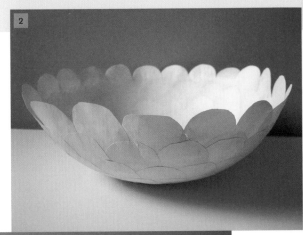

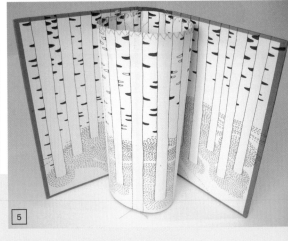

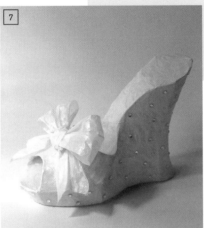

GÉRALDINE GONZALEZ

6 Cigogne sculpture/installation
Papier-mâché.

7 Mule sculpture
Papier-mâché.

SIBA SAHABI

8 Sculpture
Paper, 'Tea Dance' series.

9 & 10 Sculptures
Paper, 'Bucchero' series.

Paper and Woodwork

NIC WEBB

1 Spoons, forks, slice
American walnut.

2 Untitled bowl
Ash.

3 Coral bowl
Yew.

ANNICK KRASNOPOLSKI – LES RECYCLÉS

4 Racket mirror
Tennis racket, mirror.

SUSAN DWYER

5 Gold Point Vessel
Papier-mâché, acrylic paint and gold leaf.

6 Bowls
Set of two, papier-mâché, with polyurethane finish.

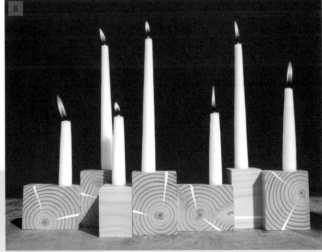

JEAN PELLE

7 Billie candle-holders
Turned fir, with a highly polished
ebonized finish.

8 Joyce candle-holders
Cross-sectioned fir, deep cracks
filled with a super-bright white filling.

9 Dorit candle-holders
Warm-hued poplar, with 24-carat
gold leaf.

Stationery

JURIANNE MATTER

1 Blom
15 easy pop-out paper flowers, with 4.5m florist's wire.

2 Angels
Seven flatpacked paper angel cards, each with a different pattern.

3 Wish Boats
Eight paper boat sheets, each with a different pattern.

BAILEY DOESN'T BARK

4 Ruler
Notebook, 48 lined pages, recycled natural white paper, soy-based ink.

5 Happy Holidays
Four blank fold cards and brown envelopes, recycled paper, soy-based ink.

SERROTE

6 Caderno Lenha
Letterpress notebook.

7 12 Cartões
Set of twelve printed cards in letterpress.

8 Liga dos Amigos do Jardim Botânico
Letterpress notebook.

9 A Vida Portuguesa
Letterpress notebook.

CLAIRE COLES

10 Gift cards
Pack of five printed gift cards with five green envelopes.

FRIC DE MENTOL

11 Lollipop Girl
Travel pocket journal, with gocco-printed Moleskine cover.

12 Friendship
Travel pocket journal, with gocco-printed Moleskine cover.

Tableware

STUDIO KIKI VAN EIJK

1 Soft Vessel
White porcelain.

2 Celadon Plate (Deer)
Porcelain.

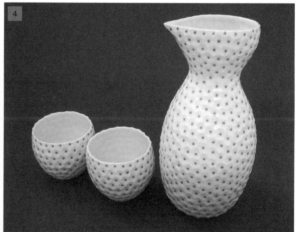

8

7

9

KUKO IWAMOTO

Coloured Guinomi cups
Porcelain.

Nucleolus sake set
Porcelain.

Nucleolus Pofu Blue teapot
Porcelain.

Kinorhyncha beakers
Porcelain.

MEL ROBSON

**Little Uns (polka dot) cups
and saucers**
Slipcast porcelain, with inlay.

Fortitude bowl
Slipcast porcelain, with decals.

**Blackbird/Bird on a Wire
wall beakers**
Slipcast porcelain, with decals.

SUTURNO

**0 Magnolia Pattern cups
and saucers**
Ceramic, with decals.

10

BAILEY DOESN'T BARK

1 Dots cup and saucer
23-carat gold dots on natural white
porcelain, 'Dots' collection.

2 Tea Bag mug and saucer
Natural white porcelain.

LAURA STRASSER

3 Mosaïque service
Porcelain.

4 Tiger vessel
Porcelain.

5 Milkmoments bowls
Porcelain, co-created with Milia
Seyppel.

SISSEL WATHNE

**6 Mrs Ingeborg, Miss Ellen, Little
Marie and Old Betty eggcup and
spoon sets**
Porcelain.

KRASZNAI

7 Tall vase
Porcelain, 'Arms&Crafts' series.

8 Bowl
Porcelain, 'Arms&Crafts' series.

9 Jugs/vases
Porcelain, 'Arms&Crafts' series.

WAUW DESIGN

10 Services
Porcelain, 'Raw' and 'Songlines'
collections.

NINAINVORM

1 Plates
Vintage porcelain, with decals.

2 Pitcher
Porcelain, with decals.

3 Apple box
Porcelain, with decals.

4 Display plate
Porcelain, with decals.

CLAIRE COLES

5 Mugs
Bone china with digital-transfer
floral wallpaper design.

6

7

9

10

SARAH CIHAT

6 Teal Doe No. 2 plate
Porcelain, 'Rehabilitated Dishware'
series.

7 Red Hawk plate
Porcelain, 'Rehabilitated Dishware'
series.

8 Red Fleur plate
Porcelain, 'Rehabilitated Dishware'
series.

9 Lime Doe No. 2 plate
Porcelain, 'Rehabilitated Dishware'
series.

LARS RANK

10 Dots tableware
Porcelain.

Textiles

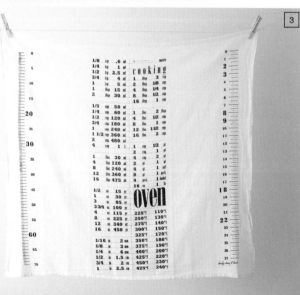

PUDDIN'HEAD

1 Antlers artwork
Belgian linen, with embroidered
rosettes.

2 Poppy design cushion
Cotton, in Atticus colour.

BAILEY DOESN'T BARK

3 Useful Towel
White cotton floursack, hand-printed
with conversions and measurements

4 Ants On My Cushion
Soft hand-printed cotton.

SUTURNO

5 Espiga 1 & 2 cushions
Hand-printed cotton, 'Tramas'
collection.

JEN DESCHÊNES

6 Cushion
Hand-screenprinted and
embroidered silk satin dévoré.

7 Sergeant cushion
Hand-screenprinted and
embroidered silk satin dévoré.

**8 Man with Hand and Rose
cushion**
Hand-embroidered vintage cotton.

DEPEAPA

9 Glasses cushion cover
Hand-printed cotton.

1

2

3

4

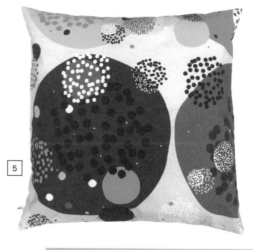

5

LENA LEVCHENKO

1, 2 & 3 Cushions
Handmade with native Ukrainian
embroideries in cotton and viscose.

ATELIER R. BERNIER

4 Ani Moose cushion
Embroidered in white cotton,
'Animality' collection.

5 Zig 02 cushion
Printed cotton, 'Zig, Boom!' fabric
collection.

**6 Troph1 orange and Troph3 white
cushions**
Screenprinted French Toile de Jouy
cotton fabric, 'Trophée de Chasse'
collection.

6

7

9

8

10

11

FRIC DE MENTOL

7 The Girl Who Knitted Love lavender pillows
Hand-printed cotton, filled with fresh lavender buds.

8 Le Solitaire lavender pillows
Hand-printed cotton, filled with fresh lavender buds.

VERA JOÃO ESPINHA

9 & 10 Hot water bottles
Leftover knitted wool.

STUDIO KIKI VAN EIJK

11 Kiki Carpet Special
Handmade, with 'cross-stitched-like' rose pattern.

ELISA STROZYK

12 Wooden Carpet
Handmade, 'Wooden Textiles' series.

12

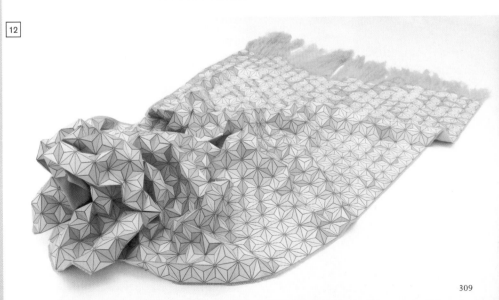

LENA LEVCHENKO

1 & 2 Shopper bags
Handmade, textile with embroidery and button details.

3 Evening bag
Handmade, textile with chain and embroidery.

ANDREA WILLIAMSON

4 Fair Isle folk hat
Lambswool.

5 Fair Isle smukks
Lambswool slippers.

6 Russian Doll pram set
Lambswool.

ANTONIA ROSSI

7 Brevi pouches
Hand-crochet, with silk fabric remnants.

ANGUS & CELESTE

8 Wrap belt
Candy red and floral fabrics, with porcelain buckle.

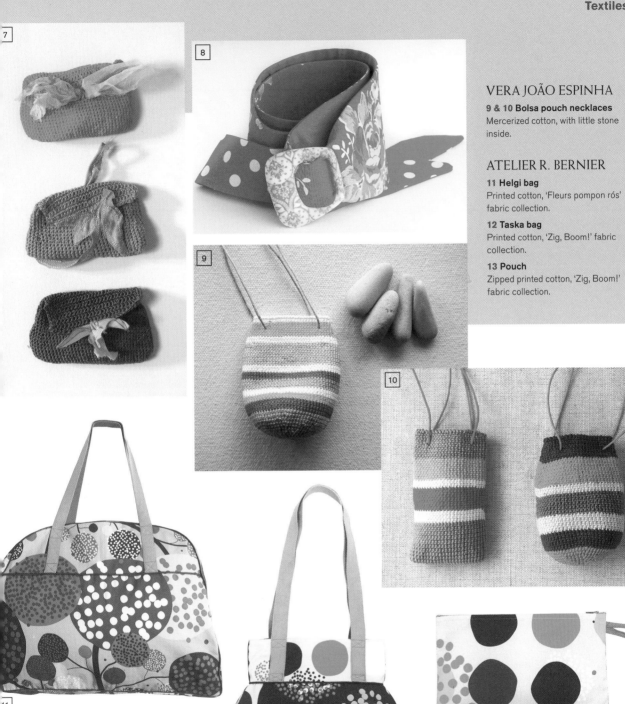

VERA JOÃO ESPINHA

9 & 10 Bolsa pouch necklaces
Mercerized cotton, with little stone inside.

ATELIER R. BERNIER

11 Helgi bag
Printed cotton, 'Fleurs pompon rós' fabric collection.

12 Taska bag
Printed cotton, 'Zig, Boom!' fabric collection.

13 Pouch
Zipped printed cotton, 'Zig, Boom!' fabric collection.

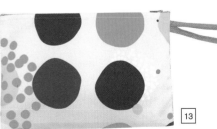

Textiles

ANN WOOD

1 Sailboat
Papier-mâché and textile, with Merry Wobbler passengers.

2 Corsage Girl
Handmade vintage fabric bird.

3 Lago Owl
Handmade with antique Japanese textiles.

DEPEAPA

4 Personajes dolls
Handmade, illustrated textile.

ANDREA WILLIAMSON

5 Russian Doll cushions
Lambswool.

6 Hang About Horse ornaments
Lambswool.

ALEXA LIXFELD

7 (clockwise from top left) Pasan, Hansitha, Ikesh, Sabana and Imesha dolls
Handwoven organic cotton.

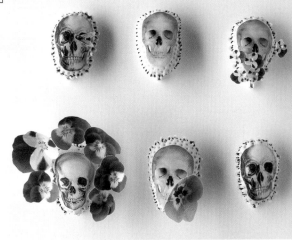

LYNDIE DOURTHE

1, 2 & 3 Vanités brooches
Printed cotton, with organdie origami wrapping.

FUROR BRILLANTE

4 Embroidery on black silk satin
With black silk ruche from nineteenth-century skirt, lace, sequins, dyed tracing paper, acetate.

5 Embroidery on midnight-blue silk satin
With oilskin cotton, sequins, cup sequins, rocaille beads, tubular beads.

SUTURNO

6 Las Casas scarf
Hand-stitched silk, in brick red.

7 Las Casas scarf
Hand-stitched silk, in grey blue.

DUVELLEROY

8 Chiffon fan
Half-moon-shaped, black organza
leaf cover, veil of changing blue-
black muslin embroidered with black
and silvery sequins, guards and
sticks in carbon fibre.

9 Black Balloon fan
Fontage-shaped, leaf in silk organza
embroidered with a bow made of a
thousand glittering black sequins,
guards and sticks in ebony.

10 Midnight Bird fan
Half-moon-shaped, leaf made of
eighteen midnight-blue ostrich
feathers and an origami of silk
muslin, guards and sticks in naturally
green mother-of-pearl.

Resources

Recommended shops

The unique, the whimsical, the desirable, the exceptional.... These addresses are among my favourite places to visit, be it to shop, indulge, treat someone or simply recharge my mind with creative and inspirational sights. The list is highly subjective and non-exhaustive.

Chicago

Alphabetique
701 West Armitage Avenue,
Chicago, IL 60614
Tel +1 (312) 751 2920
A really special place to source great stationery, beautiful paper and other handmade gifts.

London

DARKROOM
www.darkroomlondon.com
52 Lamb's Conduit St,
London WC1N 3LL
Tel +44 (0)20 7831 7244
The place to go for contemporary, stylish independent designers' creations.

Luna & Curious
http://lunaandcurious.blogspot.com
24–26 Calvert Avenue,
London E2 7JP
Tel +44 (0)20 3222 0034
Whimsical, poetic collection of womenswear and home ornaments.

New York

ABC Home
888 & 881 Broadway at
East 19th Street, New York,
NY 10003
Tel +1 (212) 473 3000
The go-to place for exquisite and desirable homewares and decorative wonders.

De Vera
www.deveraobjects.com
1 Crosby Street, New York,
NY 10013
Tel +1 (212) 625 0838 and
26 East 81st Street,
New York, NY 10028
Tel +1 (212) 288 2288

Cabinet of wonders: a finely curated selection of antiques and exquisite luxurious curiosities.

Paris

107RIVOLI (the boutique at the Musée des Arts Décoratifs)
www.lesartsdecoratifs.fr
107, rue de Rivoli, 75001 Paris
Tel +33 (0)1 42 60 64 94
A great resource for unique creations, design books and a strong selection of ceramic and glass wares.

7L
7, rue de Lille, 75007 Paris
Tel +33 (0)1 42 92 03 58
No wonder this selection of books on art, lifestyle, photography and design is so amazing: the maestro behind the venture is Karl Lagerfeld.

Astier de Villatte
www.astierdevillatte.com
173, rue Saint-Honoré, 75001 Paris
Tel +33 (0)1 42 60 74 13
Own-brand ceramic tableware collection with a few extra wonders especially curated for this shop.

Centre Commercial
www.centrecommercial.cc
2, rue de Marseille, 75010 Paris
Tel +33 (0)1 42 02 26 08
Concept store of the future: desirable fashion labels, vintage objects and eco-friendly Brazilian footwear/accessory brand, Veja.

Chocolaterie/Salon de Thé Jacques Genin
133, rue de Turenne, 75003 Paris
Tel +33 (0)1 45 77 29 01
Sit in the modern salon and enjoy rare Chinese teas and delicious pastries and chocolates made in-house.

French Touche
www.frenchtouche.com
1, rue Jacquemont, 75017 Paris
Tel +33 (0)1 42 63 31 36
The anti-mass-retail-chain concept: unique, whimsical treats by independent designers in fashion, stationery, jewelry and homewares; nothing is overexposed.

Gallery S. Bensimon
www.bensimon.com/fr/gallery
SB_annexe.htm
111, rue de Turenne, 75003 Paris
Tel +33 (0)1 42 74 50 77

Desirable products from independent designers.

Le Petit Atelier de Paris
www.lepetitatelierdeparis.com
31, rue de Montmorency,
75003 Paris
Tel +33 (0)1 44 54 91 40
Charming handmade porcelain accessories and tablewares.

Miller et Bertaux
www.milleretbertaux.com
17, rue Ferdinand Duval,
75004 Paris
Tel +33 (0)1 42 78 28 39
Alongside Miller et Bertaux's own womenswear, candles and fragrances is a fantastic selection of out-of-the-ordinary objects and creations.

Neighbours
www.neighbours.fr
30, rue des Petites Écuries,
75010 Paris
Tel +33 (0)9 81 86 06 60
A splendid display of unique homewares and accessories: you may want to buy everything.

Ostentatoire
www.ostentatoire-paris.com
11 bis, rue Elzévir, 75003 Paris
Tel +33 (0)1 42 74 53 03
The best selection of up-and-coming fancy jewelry designers.

Rue Hérold
www.rueherold.com
8, rue Hérold, 75001 Paris
Tel +33 (0)1 42 33 66 56
Quality furnishing and clothing fabrics by the metre, at affordable prices, in a superbly stylish environment.

UAH
www.uah-paris.com
62, rue de l'Arbre Sec, 75001 Paris
Tel +33 (0)1 42 33 66 66
Food store + gallery + tableware = the best creative Asian shop in Paris.

Sydney

David met Nicole
www.davidmetnicole.com
382 Cleveland Street, Surry Hills,
Sydney, NSW 2010
Tel +61 (0)2 9698 7416
British vintage wonders and curiosities in an Ali Babaesque cave-like little shop.

Kaleidoscope Gallery
www.kaleidoscope-gallery.com
84 William Street, Paddington,
Sydney, NSW 2021
Tel +61 (0)2 9358 6992
A pocket-sized gallery that cleverly promotes up-and-coming artists.

Koskela showroom and shop
www.koskela.com.au
Level 1, Imperial Slacks Building,
91 Campbell Street, Surry Hills,
Sydney, NSW 2010
Tel +61 (0)2 9280 0999
A homage to Australian craft: furniture, accessories, homewares books, all selected with great flair.

Patisse
www.patisse.com.au
Shop G01, PYD Building,
197 Young St, Waterloo,
Sydney, NSW 2017
Tel +61 (0)2 9690 0665
Great place for an easy yet delicious lunch or a takeaway patisserie treat.

Planet Furniture
www.planetfurniture.com.au
114 Commonwealth Street,
Surry Hills, Sydney, NSW 2010
Tel +61 (0)2 9211 5959
Hardwood stylish furniture, but above all a beautiful selection of contemporary ceramic pieces.

The Society Inc
www.thesocietyinc.com.au
18 Stewart Street, Paddington,
Sydney, NSW 2021
Tel +61 (0)2 9331 1592
Inspirational shop and evolving gallery by freelance stylist and interior designer, Sibella Court.

Tokyo

Classico
www.classico-life.com
Yamaoka Bdg 102, 2-5-22 Yanaka
Taitou-Ku, Tokyo 110-0001
Tel +81 (0)3 3823 7622
A great, tasteful combination of antique Japanese artifacts and casual menswear.

Spiral Market
www.spiral.co.jp
5-6-23 Minami Aoyama,
Minato-Ku, Tokyo 107-0062
Tel +81 (0)3 3498 5792
International selection of utilitarian but gorgeous design pieces: baby, home and tablewares, jewelry, stationery, accessories.

Recommended websites & blogs

Some great resources to keep track of the independent artisan/design scene:

www.designspongeonline.com
www.finelittleday.com
www.ignant.de
www.irinagraewe.de
www.mooshpie.co.uk
www.notcot.org
www.phoebeeason.com
www.poppytalkhandmade.com
www.story-thestore.com
www.supermarketsarah.com
http://bloesem.blogs.com/bloesem
http://blog.sub-studio.com
http://dossier37.tumblr.com
http://seesawdesigns.blogspot.com
http://studiofludd.blogspot.com

The artisans' websites

Alexa Lixfeld
www.alexalixfeld.com
Andrea Williamson
www.andreawilliamson.co.uk
Angus & Celeste
www.angusandceleste.com.au
Ann Wood
www.annwoodhandmade.com,
www.annwood.net/blog
Anna Atterling
www.annaatterling.se
Anna Emilia Laitinen
www.annaemilia.com,
http://annaemilia.bigcartel.com
Anne Holman
www.anneholman.com, http://
anneholmanart.blogspot.com,
www.etsy.com/shop/anneholman,
http://supermarkethq.com/
designer/3800/collection/500
**Annick Krasnopolski – Les
recyclés** www.les-recycles.eu

Antonia Rossi
antomoon@inwind.it
Atelier Polyhedre
www.polyhedre.com, http://
atelierpolyhedre.blogspot.com
Atelier R. Bernier
www.atelier-rbernier.fr,
www.atelier-rbernier.fr/blog
Atsuko Ishii
www.atsuko-ishii.com
Aurélie William Levaux
aureliewilliam@yahoo.fr,
www.5c.be/book.php?id=58
Bailey Doesn't Bark
www.baileydoesntbark.com
Blanka Šperková
http://amanita-design.net/
blankasperkova
Cathrine Kullberg
www.cathrinekullberg.com
Cecilia Levy www.cecilialevy.com
Chizu Kobayashi
www.chizkobject.com, www.flickr.
com/photos/21630708@N04
Claire Coles
www.clairecolesdesign.co.uk
Cynthia Vardhan
www.cynthiavardhan.com,
http://www.etsy.com/shop/
cynthiavardhan
Depeapa www.depeapa.com,
www.flickr.com/photos/depeapa,
http://depeapashop-wood.
blogspot.com, http://depeapashop.
blogspot.com
Duvelleroy
www.duvelleroy.fr
Eileen Gatt
www.eileengatt.co.uk
Elisa Strozyk
www.elisastrozyk.de
Esque Studio
www.esque-studio.com
Fric de Mentol
http://dropesdementol.blogspot.
com, www.etsy.com/shop/
fricdementol
Furor Brillante
http://furorbrillante.blogspot.com
Géraldine Gonzalez
www.geraldinegonzalez.com
Hanna af Ekström
www.hannaafekstrom.com, http://
hannaafekstrom.blogspot.com

Ikuko Iwamoto
www.ikukoi.co.uk, http://
ikukoceramic.blogspot.com
JAMESPLUMB
www.jamesplumb.co.uk
Janis Heezen
www.janisheezen.ch
Jean Pelle www.jeanpelle.com,
www.etsy.com/shop/jeanpelle
Jen Deschênes
www.jendeschenes.co.uk,
www.jendeschenes.blogspot.com
Jurianne Matter
www.juriannematter.nl, http://
juriannematter.blogspot.com
Krasznai www.krasznai.co.uk
Kristin Lora www.kristinlora.com
Kristina Klarin
http://kristinaklarin.blogspot.com,
http://kristinaklarin.bigcartel.com
Lars Rank www.rank.dk, www.
youlittleteapot.com, www.rank-yum.
com
Laura Strasser
www.laura-strasser.de
Lena Levchenko
www.nabnable.com
Lyndie Dourthe
http://lyndiedourthe.monsite-
orange.fr, http://lyndiedourthe.
blogspot.com, http://lyndie
dourtheshop.monsite-orange.fr
Manon Gignoux
www.manon-gignoux.com
Maria Jauhiainen
maria.jauhiainen@talk21.com
Marie Christophe
www.mariechristophe.com
Mel Robson
http://feffakookan.blogspot.com
Melanie Bilenker
www.melaniebilenker.com
Nathalie Choux
www.nathaliechoux.com,
http://oeuf-egg.blogspot.com
Nic Webb www.nicwebb.com
Ninainvorm
http://ninainvorm.punt.nl,
http://www.etsy.com/shop/
ninainvorm
Nora Rochel
www.nora-rochel.de

Paula Juchem
www.paulajuchem.com,
www.paola.biz/paula.html,
http://mona-loca.blogspot.com
Puddin'head
www.puddinhead.com.au
Rohan Eason
www.rohaneason.com
Rothschild & Bickers
www.rothschildbickers.com
Sarah Cihat www.sarahcihat.com
Serrote www.serrote.com
**Severija Inčirauskaitė-
Kriaunevičienė** www.severija.lt
Sia Mai www.siamai.dk
Siba Sahabi www.sibasahabi.com
Silke Decker www.silkedecker.de
Sissel Wathne
www.sisselwathne.com
Soojin Kang www.soojinkang.net
Sophie Cook
www.sophiecook.com
String Gardens
www.stringgardens.com
Studio Kiki van Eijk
www.kikiworld.nl
Studio mhl www.studio-mhl.com,
http://studiomhl.blogspot.com
Susan Dwyer
www.susandwyer.com,
http://upintheairsomewhere.com
Susie Cowie
www.susiecowie.com
SuTurno
www.suturno.net, http://suturno-
diario.blogspot.com, www.suturno.
net/shop
Suzie Stanford
www.suziestanford.com
Vera João Espinha
http://perdi-o-fio-a-meada.blogspot.
com, http://perdi-o-fio-a-meada-
shop.blogspot.com
Wauw Design
www.wauw-design.dk
Wiebke Meurer
www.wiebkemeurer.com
Xenia Taler www.xeniataler.com

Picture Credits

Illustrations

Leslie Grima
grima.leslie@gmail.com
pp. 6–7, 248–9, 254–5, 266–7, 270–71, 272–3, 284–5, 290–91, 294–5, 298–9, 300–01, 306–7

Image quality control

Helen Brooke
www.maverickdesigntribe.com.au

Photographs

Alexa Lixfeld p. 8 no. 1, p. 9 nos 2 & 3 Mirjam Fruscella (www.fruscella.de); p. 9 no. 4 Deirdre Rooney (www.deirdrerooney. com); p. 9 no. 5, p. 254 nos 4 & 5 Benne Ochs (www.benneochs.de); p. 313 no. 7 Annika Lübbe (www.llce-design.com); all other photos courtesy of Alexa Lixfeld

Andrea Williamson p. 12 nos 4 & 6 Dodie Williamson; p. 310 no. 4 Mark Sinclair (www.phatsheep.co.uk); p. 310 no. 5, p. 313 no. 6 John Coutts (www. couttsphotos.com); all other photos courtesy of Andrea Williamson

Angus & Celeste p. 15 no. 3, p. 16 nos 4 & 5, p. 17 no. 6, p. 261 nos 6, 7, 8, 9 & 10, p. 272 nos 1, 2, 3 & 4, p. 311 no. 8 Jo Duck Photography (www.joduck.com); all other photos courtesy of Keir Angus MacDonald/ Angus & Celeste

Ann Wood all photos courtesy of Ann Wood

Anna Atterling p. 2, p. 22 no. 1, p. 24 no. 5 Lisa Fält; p. 23 no. 3 Ivar Sviestins (www. sviestins.com); p. 25 nos 7 & 8 Anders Freudendahl (www.andersfreudendahl.se); all other photos courtesy of Anna Atterling

Anna Emilia Laitinen p. 27 no. 5 Jani Kalevi Laitinen (www.kohtalo.com); all other photos courtesy of Anna Emilia Laitinen

Anne Holman p. 28 no. 1, p. 29 nos 3 & 4, p. 280 nos 3 & 5 Stephanie Bair-Garant (http://stephaniebairgarant.blogspot.com); p. 28 no. 2, p. 280 nos 2 & 4 Aline Yamada (http://yumiyumistudio.blogspot.com); all other photos courtesy of Anne Holman

Annick Krasnopolski – Les Recyclés p. 32 no. 1, p. 278 nos 1 & 2, p. 296 no. 4 Aude Frère (http://galerie-yunnan.blogspot. com); p. 32 no. 2 Véronique Larrue (vero. larrue@laposte.net); p. 33 nos 3 & 4 Carole Liogier (caroleliogier@gmail.com)

Antonia Rossi p. 34 no. 1, p. 36 nos 6 & 8, p. 37 no. 9, p. 277 nos 9 & 10, p. 311 no. 7 Studio Eikon (www.studioeikon.com); p. 35 no. 2, p. 36 no. 7, p. 37 nos 10 & 11 Chizu Kobayashi (www.chizkobject.com); p. 35 nos 3, 4 & 5 Sonja Mehner (www. sonjamehner.com)

Atelier Polyhedre all photos courtesy of Atelier Polyhedre

Atelier R. Bernier p. 42 no. 1, p. 43 no. 3, p. 44 no. 7, p. 266 nos 3, 4 & 5 Jérémy Lowinsky (jeremy.lowinsky@gmail.com); all other photos courtesy of Romain Bernier/ Atelier R. Bernier

Atsuko Ishii all photos by Lyndie Dourthe (http://lyndiedourthe.monsite-orange.fr)

Aurélie William Levaux all photos by La cinquième couche (www.5c.be)

Bailey Doesn't Bark all photos by Ballyscanlon (www.ballyscanlon.com)

Blanka Šperková all photos by Jakub Dvorsky (www.amanitadesign.com)

Cathrine Kullberg p. 58 no. 1 Simon Skreddernes; p. 59 no. 3 Espen Røyseland; p. 284 no. 1 Line Böhmer Lökken; all other photos courtesy of Cathrine Kullberg

Cecilia Levy p. 60 no. 1, p. 61 nos 2, 3 & 4, p. 63 no. 9, p. 294 no. 1 Ann-Sofi Rosenkvist (www.annsofirosenkvist.se); all other photos courtesy of Cecilia Levy

Chizu Kobayashi all photos courtesy of Chizu Kobayashi

Claire Coles p. 68 no. 1, p. 69 nos 2 & 3, p. 71 nos 6, 7 & 8, p. 274 nos 1 & 2, p. 299 no. 10, p. 304 no. 5 Sussie Ahlburg (www. sussieahlburg.com); p. 70 nos 4 & 5 Karin Berndl (www.karinberndl.com)

Cynthia Vardhan all photos by Brandon L. Jones (www.brandonljones.com)

Depeapa all photos by Argider Aparicio San Felices (www.argiderphoto.com)

Duvelleroy p. 78 nos 1 & 2, p. 79 no. 4, p. 80 no. 6, p. 81 nos 8 & 9, p. 315 no. 10 Lyndie Dourthe (http://lyndiedourthe. monsite-orange.fr); p. 80 no. 7, p. 315 nos 8 & 9 Grégory Finck (www.gregfinck.com); all other photos courtesy of Duvelleroy

Eileen Gatt p. 83 nos 2, 3 & 4, p. 282 nos 1, 2 & 3, p. 293 nos 7, 8 & 9 Ewen Weatherspoon (www.ewphoto.co.uk); all other photos courtesy of Eileen Gatt

Elisa Strozyk all photos by Sebastian Neeb (www.sebastianneeb.de)

Esque Studio all photos by Boone Speed (www.boonespeed.com)

Fric de Mentol all photos courtesy of Ana Raimundo/Fric de Mentol

Furor Brillante all photos by Lyndie Dourthe (http://lyndiedourthe.monsite-orange.fr)

Géraldine Gonzalez all photos courtesy of Géraldine Gonzalez

Hanna af Ekström all photos by Henrik Linden (www.coffeeblack-music.com)

Ikuko Iwamoto all photos courtesy of Ikuko Iwamoto

JAMESPLUMB p. 106 no. 1, p. 109 nos 9, 10 & 11 courtesy of Hostem (www. hostem.co.uk); p. 106 no. 2, p. 107 nos 4 & 5, p. 108 nos 7 & 8, p. 268 nos 2, 3 & 4, p. 286 no. 2 Danilo Capasso (www. danilocapasso.eu); p. 107 nos 3 & 6 Andrew Meredith (www.meredithphoto. com)

Janis Heezen all photos by Frank Blaser (www.frankblaser.ch)

Jean Pelle all photos courtesy of Jean Pelle

Jen Deschênes p. 116 nos 1, 2 & 4, p. 117 no. 5, p. 307 no. 8 Fin Macrae (www.finmacrae.com); p. 116 no. 3 Iain Ferguson (www.thewriteimage.co.uk); p. 268 no. 1, p. 307 nos 6 & 7 Ali Berardelli (mail@aliberardelli.co.uk)

Jurianne Matter p. 120 no. 6 Simone van den Berg (www.junglefrog.com); p. 298 nos 2 & 3 Heidi de Wit (www.h-en-k.nl/joomla); all other photos courtesy of Jurianne Matter

Krasznai all photos by Artur Muñoz (www. arturmunoz.com)

Kristin Lora p. 124 nos 1, 2 & 3, p. 125 no. 4, p. 127 nos 7, 8, 9 & 10, p. 283 nos 8, 9 & 10 Sara Stathas (www.sarastathas.com); p. 126 nos 5 & 6 Marian Miller; all other photos courtesy of Kristin Lora

Kristina Klarin all photos courtesy of Kristina Klarin

Lars Rank p. 130 no. 1, pp. 132–33 no. 5, p. 133 nos 6 & 7, p. 262 nos 3 & 4, p. 287 nos 6 & 7 Ole Akhøj (www. oleakhoej.dk); p. 131 no. 3, p. 263 nos 5 & 6 Martin Daugaard (www.martindaugaard. dk); all other photos courtesy of Lars Rank

Laura Strasser p. 135 no. 3 Claudia Neuhaus (www.claudianeuhaus.com); all other photos courtesy of Laura Strasser

Lena Levchenko all photos courtesy of Lena Levchenko

Lyndie Dourthe all photos courtesy of Lyndie Dourthe

Manon Gignoux p. 142 no. 1 Makiko Takehara (www.r-g-m.net); p. 142 no. 2, p. 143 no. 3, p. 144 nos 4, 5 & 6, p. 145 no. 9, p. 320 Lyndie Dourthe (http://lyndie dourthe.monsite-orange.fr); all other photos courtesy of Manon Gignoux

Maria Jauhiainen all photos courtesy of Maria Jauhiainen

Marie Christophe p. 148 nos 1 & 2, p. 149 no. 4, p. 151 no. 8, p. 253 nos 5, 6 & 7, p. 288 nos 1, 2, 3, 4 & 5 Arnaud Meyer (www.arnaudmeyer.fr); p. 149 no. 3, p. 150 nos 5 & 6, p. 151 no. 7 Michel Figuet (www.michelfiguet.fr)

Mel Robson all photos courtesy of Mel Robson

Melanie Bilenker all photos courtesy of Melanie Bilenker

Nathalie Choux all photos courtesy of Nathalie Choux

Nic Webb all photos by Michael Harvey (www.michaelharveyphoto.com)

Ninainvorm all photos courtesy of Nina van de Goor/Ninainvorm

Nora Rochel p. 166 no. 1, p. 167 no. 5, p. 276 no. 1 Janusch Tschech (www.janusch-tschech.com); p. 166 no. 2, p. 167 nos 3, 4, 6 & 7, p. 259 nos 9, 10 & 11, p. 276 no. 2 Sebastian Lang (www.seb-newton.com); p. 259 no. 8 Petra Jaschke

Paula Juchem all photos by Ruy Teixeira (www.ruyteixeira.com)

Puddin'head all photos by Sam McAdam (www.sammcadam.com)

Rohan Eason p. 174 no. 1 Eva Edsjo (www.evaedsjo.com); p. 174 no. 2 Michael Eason; all other photos courtesy of Rohan Eason

Rothschild & Bickers p. 176 no. 1, p. 178 no. 4, p. 179 nos 6 & 7, p. 289 nos 6, 7, 8, 9 & 10 Simon Camper Photography (www.simoncamper.com); p. 177 nos 2 & 3, p. 178 no. 5, p. 179 nos 8 & 9 Paul Beggy (www.paulbeggyphotography.co.uk)

Sarah Cihat p. 180 no. 1 Alick Crossley (www.alickcrossley.com); p. 181 no. 2 Lorena Barrezueta (www.lorenabarrezueta.com); p. 181 no. 4 Frederick Bouchardy (www.joyastudio.com); p. 182 no. 7 Marc Grant; p. 264 no. 6 Julia Kots (www.felisrufus.com); all other photos courtesy of Sarah Cihat

Serrote all photos courtesy of Nuno Neves/Serrote

Severija Inčirauskaitė-Kriaunevičienė all photos courtesy of Severija Inčirauskaitė-Kriaunevičienė

Sia Mai p. 188 no. 1, p. 271 nos 6 & 7 Ole Akhøj (www.oleakhoej.dk); p. 188 nos 2 & 3, p. 189 no. 5, p. 271 nos 5 & 8 Ole Victor (www.ole.victor.se); p. 189 no. 4 Sia Mai

Siba Sahabi p. 190 nos 1 & 2 Annemarijne Bax (www.annemarijnebax.nl); p. 191 nos 3 & 4, p. 192 no. 5, p. 193 no. 6, p. 295 nos 8, 9 & 10 Karin Nussbaumer (www.karinnussbaumer.com)

Silke Decker p. 195 no. 2 Monika Schedler (www.hellauf.de); p. 195 no. 3 Vincent Schrive; p. 196 nos 4 & 5, p. 197 nos 6 & 7, p. 255 nos 6 & 7 Natalie Williams (www.nataliewilliams.de); all other photos courtesy of Silke Decker

Sissel Wathne p. 198 no. 1, p. 199 no. 4 Sigrid Espelien (www.sigridespelien.com); p. 200 nos 7, 8 & 9, p. 201 no. 10, p. 262 nos 1 & 2, p. 303 no. 6 Ole Akhøj (www.oleakhoej.dk); all other photos courtesy of Sissel Wathne

Soojin Kang p. 202 no. 1, p. 203 nos 2, 3 & 4, p. 204 nos 5 & 6, p. 205 no. 7, p. 278 no. 5, p. 279 nos 6 & 7 Markus Schroder (www.markusschroder.com); p. 267 nos 8 & 9 Ania Wawrzkowicz (www.aniawawrzkowicz.com)

Sophie Cook all photos by Ian Cook (www.iancookphotography.com)

String Gardens p. 210 no. 4 Anne Dokter (www.annedokter.com); all other photos courtesy of Fedor van der Valk/String Gardens

Studio Kiki van Eijk p. 213 no. 5, p. 269 nos 5, 6, 7 & 8 Frank Tielemans (www.franktielemans.com); p. 215 no. 8 courtesy of Secondome (www.secondome.eu); p. 215 nos 9 & 10, p. 271 no. 9 Francesco Ferruzzi; p. 254 no. 1 Ruy Teixeira (www.ruyteixeira.com); p. 300 no. 1 Serena Eller (www.serenaeller.com); all other photos courtesy of Studio Kiki van Eijk

Studio mhl all photos courtesy of Monique van Bruggen/Studio mhl

Susan Dwyer all photos by Ben Syverson (http://bensyverson.com)

Susie Cowie p. 222 nos 1 & 2, p. 224 nos 5 & 6, p. 225 nos 7 & 9 Lyndie Dourthe (http://lyndiedourthe.monsite-orange.fr); p. 250 nos 1 & 2, p. 280 no. 1 Peartree Digital (www.peartreedigital.com); all other photos courtesy of Susie Cowie and Katie McInnes

SuTurno p. 226 no. 1, p. 301 no. 10 Manolo Yllera (www.manoloyllera.com); p. 307 no. 5, p. 315 nos 6 & 7 Rosa Veloso (www.rosaveloso.es); all other photos courtesy of SuTurno

Suzie Stanford p. 228 no. 1, p. 266 nos 1 & 2 Sharyn Cairns (www.sharyncairns.com.au); p. 229 no. 2, p. 230 nos 3, 4 & 5, p. 231 no. 6, p. 292 no. 3 Earl Carter (www.earlcarter.com.au)

Vera João Espinha p. 232 no. 2 Paulo Alves (www.behance.net/PauloFilipeAlves); p. 233 no. 3, p. 235 no. 10 Rita Espinha (www.ritaespinha.webs.com); all other photos courtesy of Vera João Espinha

Wauw Design all photos by Jakob Galtt (www.jakobgaltt.com)

Wiebke Meurer all photos courtesy of Wiebke Meurer

Xenia Taler all photos courtesy of Steven Koblinsky and Xenia Taler

Acknowledgments

It takes a community to build a city, and in the same way it takes a cluster of talent and support to create a project such as a book.

First and foremost, I would like to thank everyone at Thames & Hudson, especially Jamie Camplin, who believed in me and offered me this joyful opportunity.

I would also like to thank warmly the friends who instilled their faith in me, who offered me feedback and guidance, and who contributed their time and expertise – Helen Brooke, Kelly Doust, Lyndie Dourthe, Romain Bernier – and, of course, with all my love, the dear people who have given me unflagging support all along and far beyond – Marie-Françoise, André, Mark, Christine and Ludivine.

Last but not least, this book would not be what it is without the unique skills, unbridled creativity and professional drive of the seventy-five great talents who honoured me with their participation.

About the author

Olivier Dupon began his career at Christian Dior. He expanded his expertise in the fields of fashion and lifestyle by working as a buyer and product manager for several large retail companies before opening his own boutique. Based in Australia, he now scouts international markets in search of design/art/craft objects and projects to feature on his blog, www.Dossier37.tumblr.com.

left Textile composition by Manon Gignoux.